The Joe Namath Story

Joe Namath is the most exciting and controversial sports figure in America today. Ever since he started playing football for money—and even before—Namath has been making headlines. Now he's lived one of the great comeback stories in sports history. After missing most of two seasons with injuries, Joe returned to the New York Jets' lineup on a fulltime basis in 1972—and reclaimed his position as the top quarterback in the National Football League, a status he has held since he led the downrated Jets to the Super Bowl title in 1969 in one of the most incredible upsets the sports world ever has witnessed.

This revealing book tells the story of Namath's meteoric rise to the top of the pro football world. It also provides intimate glimpses into the private life of the after-dark celebrity who wears a mink coat, owns a llama rug, sleeps in an oval, satin-sheeted bed, and stars in motion pictures— the high-living, ex-small town boy whom his fans (especially the girls) call "Broadway Joe."

Namath is, unquestionably, the hottest personality in the sports world—and the most sought after. He appears in more varied, and highly rated commercials than any other star in sports. His outside interests net him nearly $250,000 a year to go along with his $250,000 salary from the Jets, making him the highest paid pro football player in the long history of the game.

Sportswriter Larry Bortstein has followed the Namath story from its inception and his inside account of Joe's journey up the glory road—from Beaver Falls to Broadway, with stops in Hollywood and Miami—is based on personal knowledge, fresh research and interviews with the white-shoed wonder, Number 12, himself.

the SUPERJOE joe namath story

revised edition
by larry bortstein

tempo books

GROSSET & DUNLAP

A National General Company

Publishers   New York

Acknowledgments

The author wishes to acknowledge the following for their cooperation and assistance in preparing the original edition of this work: Frank Ramos, publicity director of the New York Jets, and his assistant, Jim Trecker; Harold Rosenthal, publicity director of the American Football Conference; Carroll (Beano) Cook of the American Broadcasting Company; Phil Pepe of the sports department of the New York *Daily News,* and Pete Axthelm, sports editor of *Newsweek.*

Contents

1. Number One Quarterback

HE stands, a gimpy-kneed colossus, atop the pro football world. No sports celebrity of modern times has achieved the adulation, the hero worship—or the contempt—heaped upon Joe Willie Namath of the New York Jets.

And probably no other performer in all the years of pro football could accomplish the kind of comeback achieved by this same Namath during the 1972 National Football League season.

In many minds, Joe was the number one quarterback in the game during the 1970 and 1971 seasons—when he could play. But Namath missed most of both seasons with injuries. In 1970 he appeared in only the first five games of the regular campaign before he suffered a broken wrist. In 1971, his wrist fully healed, Joe was the sensation of New York's training camp. But he was knocked out for the first 10 games of the regular competition when he was felled by ferocious Detroit Lion tacklers in the first exhibition game and wrenched an already shaky knee.

Late in the 1971 season, shortly after his return to the gridiron wars, Namath served notice that he was still the dominant passer in the sport: with a display of throwing and play-calling that left his opponents dazed, Joe nearly pitched the Jets to a tremendous upset victory over the powerful and playoff-bound San Francisco 49ers.

In 1972, though the Jets finished a distant second (seven wins, seven losses) in the final standings of the American Conference's Eastern Division—behind eventual Super Bowl-winning Miami—Joe led all passers in the NFL in yardage gained through the air with 2816, and tied (with Washington's Bill Kilmer) for the NFL championship in touchdown passes with 19.

En route to regaining his position as the quarterback on most All-Pro teams, Namath posted two of the most remarkable efforts in pro annals. The first of these came on the second Sunday of the 1972 campaign.

Two Weeb Ewbank disciples matched talents in an orgy of the airlanes. John Unitas of the Baltimore Colts, whom Ewbank had coached when Unitas was a young man in the NFL, shattered his own club record for completions in a single game and gained 376 yards. Namath fared even better during an all-out assault on the Colt secondary. He completed 15 of his 28 passes for six touchdowns and an unbelievable 496 yards. This averaged out to more than 33 yards per completion, and included scoring strikes of 79 and 80 yards to Rich Caster.

Joe didn't stop there. In a Monday night game at

Oakland, before a national television audience, Namath fired pass after pass through the frosty night. When he was done, he had 26 completions in 46 attempts for 403 yards. Bob Brown, a much-decorated, 280-pound offensive tackle for the Raiders, spoke of Namath in awe after the game.

"I found myself looking at the game like a fan," Brown recalled. "I was standing there on the sidelines and couldn't believe him. He was like a magician. He was unreal. He keeps his club in the game up until that man shoots the final gun in the air."

After two years of frustrating injuries, Namath's return to pro football was complete. But, despite the fact that he still moved around with the same swaggering gait that worshippers around the country had tried to emulate since Broadway Joe's entry into the game in 1965, this was in many ways a new Joe Namath. This was a Joe Namath who could say, "I pray every night when I go to bed—when I can."

It was a Joe Namath quite different from—yet in many respects exactly the same as—a young man from Beaver Falls.

2. Namath the "Natural"

If Mark Twain had lived in Beaver Falls and had known Joe Namath, nobody would have heard of Tom Sawyer.
—Beano Cook, sportswriter and publicist.

BEAVER Falls, Pennsylvania, is grass-roots America. It is the kind of place in which Tom Sawyer could have been raised. Located in the heart of western Pennsylvania, thirty miles north of Pittsburgh, there is an air of familiarity about it that such small towns (population: 16,240) have. In Beaver Falls, gentlemen still tip their hats.

But for all the gentle ways of the folks in Beaver Falls it will never be mistaken for an outpost of easy living. Nobody clips coupons in this town. It does not resemble Scarsdale or Greenwich or Great Neck for lawn-sprinklers and two-car garages and ranch-style homes. Beaver Falls is a steel-mill town.

Hulking factories squat in the Beaver Valley—industrial complexes such as Babcock and Wilcox, Republic Steel, Moltrup Steel Products and Armstrong Cork—their chimneys belching smoke all day long across the city and over the Beaver River by which the town is set.

Making steel is a tough business. In the shadow of flaming furnaces, men lift and load and wield and mold, and at the end of the day their muscles ache, their bodies drip with sweat. At the end of a lifetime, the men who work in the steel mills are bone weary from their labors.

There is money in steel, but not for the men who do the muscle work. They make a pittance of what management people earn. Theirs is a commodity that is of no particular distinction: they are bodies. In steel mills, bodies are not heavily rewarded.

So Beaver Falls in this century has drawn to it men whose only resource is their willingness to work hard. Swarms of Poles, Hungarians, Slovaks, Italians and, in later years, Negroes, emigrated there to work the ever-changing shifts in the mills. John Namath, Joe's father, came to Beaver Falls from Hungary as a kid, and saw his old man go to the mills. And not long after, John Namath followed him there.

John Namath's job was to make steel tubes for boilers. It was not the kind of toil he wished on his progeny. He and Rose Namath had five children, all of whom were athletically inclined. John Jr., 12 years older than Joe, played high school football, but without much distinction. Frank, the second born, was an aggressive lineman, good enough to earn a scholarship to the University of Kentucky. Bobby, the next born, was considered an excellent quarterback prospect, until he quit high school. Even Rita, an adopted sister, liked to throw the football around with her brothers.

In the steel country of western Pennsylvania, football was more than just a game. It was an opportunity to escape from drab prospects. That is why the football played in the high schools of the area still draws college talent scouts. The kids in western Pennsylvania play for keeps. For in football, a man whose merit is in his body is treasured far more than he would be in the mills.

No wonder, then, that so many young men from the steel country have gone on to colleges and to the professional leagues to play football. Vito (Babe) Parilli (University of Kentucky, Boston Patriots, New York Jets) was raised in Valley, eight miles from Beaver Falls. Mike Ditka is from nearby Aliquippa. Terry Hanratty, Jim Mutscheller, Joe Walton: they are only a few of the tough and hungry kids who eluded the steels mills through their abilty to play football. In the Beaver Valley, even a second-stringer from a good team sometimes gets a scholarship.

That was the heritage into which Joseph William Namath was born on May 31, 1943. And it didn't take him long to realize he wanted no part of the steel mills. "I was afraid I was going to have to spend my life there," he said. "I dreaded that. I saw my father come home tired and grimy. I hated it."

Once, Joe's father took him to the mill in which he worked. The furor of the machinery oppressed young Namath, a spirited lad even then. He never went back, and vowed he never would.

He started playing sports when he was young. "Joe was throwing a football when he was big enough to walk," remembers his mother. "His brothers, Bobby and Franklin, always got up football games in the front yard. Joe was just five and too little to play, but the boys needed a quarterback. So Joe was it."

"As a boy, Joe would play all day long," recalled John Namath. "Then he would come home at night and practice hook shots against the wall with a softball."

He learned to play tough at a young age. "He had to catch the ball or get knocked down by his brothers," the father said. "They didn't take pity on Joe."

But they did educate him. "Bobby and Franklin taught Joe to throw the ball over the telephone wires," his mother said. Joe got so he could throw the ball out of sight, and he could hit a stump from forty yards away."

As a youngster, however, Joe Namath was not the superior athlete he later was: he was too small. "I remember Joe used to come home from Little League baseball practice and tell me that the other boys were so much better then he was," his father said. "But I never let him feel sorry for himself, and neither did his brothers. I told him once to take his uniform back and give it to the manager if he didn't feel he was the best player on the field. I told him, 'If you don't have confidence, you can't do anything.' "

It was a lesson that Joe learned well. He rarely had doubts about himself after that, whatever the sport. Take football: "Joe started playing football in the Pop Warner League when he was ten or eleven," his dad remembered. "He was so small that he couldn't see his pass receivers when the linemen stood up. But even then he believed in himself."

He constantly worked to be better at sports. On Fourth Avenue in Beaver Falls, two blocks from the Namaths' little frame house, the Fame Laundry bore witness to the athletic progress of Joe and his friends. "We put so many footballs, baseballs and stones through the windows that they finally covered them over with wallboard," Namath said.

It was not Joe's only mischief. His circumstances—he lived in the Lower End, the town's poorest section—made him street-wise in a hurry. "Right near where we lived," he said, "there was a bottling plant and then a junkyard, and what we'd do was to go down to the Beaver River and pick up junk that we sold at the junkyard. Sometimes," he winked "it happened that some of the junk we sold 'em would be borrowed from the back of the junkyard and sold again at the front."

It wasn't merely junk that young Joe Willie dealt in. "I stole golf balls when I was a kid and then I lied when they asked me if I stole them, and I lied again when they asked me if I'd lied. I didn't steal 'em because I was a bad guy. I just needed the money."

He did some crazy things for money. There was the time he baited a cop by telling him that he would sneak into a Geneva College basketball game. The cop bet him a nickel that he couldn't do it.

"I got in through a window after edging along a ledge two, three stories high," Joe said. "The cop gave me my nickel and then threw me out. I had to sneak back in again."

Not all his mischief had an economic basis. Some of it was in the Tom Sawyer fashion—just for mischief's sake. Truancy. Swimming in the Beaver River. Rock fights. "Me and Benny Singleton combined gangs once," Namath told a writer, "and I was the only white boy in it. We had these hills there—Jungle Hill, which was like a jungle, and Bunny Hill, which had two paths coming down off it that looked like rabbit ears, and Tin Hill. Tin Hill was a metal dump, and when we had these rock fights and somebody was up on Tin Hill it took a war to get 'em off."

For all his derring-do, Joe Willie was still a peewee when he reached junior high school. "Gee, if I was just a little taller," he told his father, "I could see over those linemen." At 5 feet, 115 pounds, there weren't too many options. He stayed at quarterback.

Joe's parents separated before he got to high school. To ease his hurts, he focused his energies on sports. He played everything. And in the Lower End, now a predominantly Negro section, the competition was plenty tough. By the time he enrolled at Beaver Falls High School, he was a rugged performer in football, basketball and baseball.

But not rugged enough to suit varsity football coach Billy Ross in 1958, Joe's sophomore year. "He didn't even make it to summer football camp that summer," John Namath recalled. "But we kept telling him to let the coaches know he wanted to play. So he went to practice every day. He only got into one play that year, and it was on defense. But I can't believe that any other kid wanted to play as bad as he did."

Namath's persistence paid off in his junior year. Beaver Falls had a new coach, Larry Bruno. Bruno based his plans for the season on the films he viewed of Beaver Falls' '58 games. That meant that senior quarterback, Richie Neidbala, would be the starter. And Joe Willie would have to begin from scratch.

Neidbala wasn't moved out very easily. He was just too good. During the course of his career, he'd once completed 15 straight passes and shown himself so capable a performer that the college scouts queued up to offer scholarships by the end of his schoolboy years.

But for all Neidbala's skills, there was something about this growing Namath kid (5' 11", 165 pounds) that caught Bruno's eye. He had the cool and flair of a riverboat gambler, he did things like a natural athlete.

"He was one of those guys who could pick up a ping pong paddle for the first time and do well," Bruno said. "Right from the start, Joe looked like he had moves in football. He picked up things real quick, too. Show him once and he was the master of it immediately."

Still, Namath was a reserve. Not until the late stages of a losing season did Bruno begin planning for the future. And that's when Joe Willie got his chance. By the end of '59, Namath was sharing the quarterback position with Neidbala.

To be sure, he was no Johnny Unitas at this point, but he was working at it. For Joe Willie, Unitas was the paragon of what a quarterback should be. He patterned his moves after the Baltimore Colt quarterback, and even insisted on wearing jersey No. 19—Unitas' number. "A friend used to call me Joey U. for Unitas," he said.

By the time he was a senior, Namath had grown to 6' 1", 175 pounds. In his years of quarterback apprenticeship, he'd grown as a tactician, too. He hadn't sat on the bench idling his time away. He'd studied what was happening on the field for his eventual use.

It was time well spent. When he did become the starting quarterback at Beaver Falls in 1960, he impressed everybody by the way he could assess football situations. Even as a high school quarterback, he had the knack of calling automatics—plays called at the line of scrimmage based on the quarterback's "reading" of a defensive alignment. This skill was rare in a college player, never mind a schoolboy one.

But Namath had prepared himself for quarterback. And, as a result, he had developed a feeling for football disproportionate to the game experience he'd had. It was as if the game on the field was mere replay of what was in Joe's head.

What *was* in Joe's head was considered just average in the classroom, but on the football field he was a regular quiz kid. "He called 99 percent of our plays," recalled Coach Bruno. "I let him. I wasn't about to mess things up."

Joe was the leader, and he made sure his teammates knew it. In the huddle, he demanded total control of the game. He abided no interference. Once, when a player meddled with his play call, Joe went to the sidelines and said to Coach Bruno, "Get that guy out of the game."

Bruno sent in a substitute. Like Namath, he agreed that the quarterback ran the game—and nobody else. For Joe Willie, he was doing it the way Johnny U. would.

But for all Namath's acquired skills as a quarterback, Joe hardly expected Beaver Falls to be a big winner. "When the season opened in 1960," he said, "I thought it was just going to be another year. You know, win a few, lose a few."

Namath's reservations were based on the caliber of football played in the "AA" grouping of the Western Pennsylvania Interscholastic Athletic League, the league in which Beaver Falls competed. WPIAL football was tough, and the toughest and best football was played by "AA" teams. In that conference Beaver Falls was smaller than most of the "AA" schools against which it competed—just 100 students over the "A" class. After a '59 season in which the Tigers had won four, lost five and tied one, there were no indications that Beaver Falls had a powerhouse.

Namath made the difference in '60. On a team that would send most of its starters to college on scholarships, he was the best of the lot. And he showed that right away in Beaver Falls' opening game against Midland.

On the second play of the game, Namath put the ball out for his running back. The Tiger blockers crashed into the Midland defenders on straight ahead power blocking. Then Joe Willie withdrew the ball, shielded it on his hip and loped easily to the outside, to create the impression of a faked handoff.

But Namath actually *had* faked the handoff and, when the Midland tacklers discovered that the running back barrelling into their midst didn't have the football, they shouted, "Bootleg. Bootleg." And they went after Namath.

It was too late. Namath had negotiated the end and was racing downfield, like a burglar fleeing the law. He went sixty yards for the touchdown.

The skill with which Namath handled the football resulted in another touchdown in the second quarter. Again Namath slapped the football into the back's belly, only to extract it with the delicacy of a safecracker working a combination lock. And with the defense converging on the decoy, Namath sprinted off tackle for the touchdown.

Namath ran, and Namath passed. And whatever he did, the Beaver Falls attack moved. He completed 7 of 17 passes for 174 yards. The Tigers won the season opener, 43-13, and Namath won the praise of the local press—even if it did spell his name wrong. "It was Joe Nameth," reported the Beaver Falls *News-Tribune,* "who guided the Tigers with a brilliant performance."

It didn't take long for people to get the spelling right. Not the way Joe Willie was playing. In the next game against Sharon High, Namath hit on his first pass and, on the same drive, threw to end Tom Krzmienski for a touchdown. He ended up completing 8 of 9 passes for 186 yards. And Beaver Falls won, 39-7.

But it wasn't until the Fallsmen played against New Castle High that Namath received his first legitimate test. New Castle was a perennial football power, and no wonder: it had an enrollment three times that of Beaver Falls'.

Namath was not fazed. He'd learned as a kid that a winner believed in himself. "They called him the cocky high school kid," says his sister-in-law, Mrs. Edith Namath. "He was good and he knew it."

Joe Willie was so confident that when Coach Bruno asked whether his injured ankle could withstand punting duties—he was the team's kicker—Namath replied, "Don't worry, coach. It won't be necessary to kick."

Joe made good on his word. He communicated his confidence to the rest of the team, and the Tigers tore into New Castle. On the opening drive, Namath moved the team . . . all the way for a touchdown.

Beaver Falls kept scoring. Namath ran for a touchdown, passed to Krzmienski for a touchdown, pitched out for two more touchdowns. For three quarters, Beaver Falls could not be stopped. It scored every time it had the football. In all, Namath completed 9 of 13 passes for 183 yards and ran for 63 yards in leading his team to a 39-0 victory.

The confidence Namath showed was not limited to the football field. Off the field, he was a jaunty figure in his mod pants, beret and sun glasses—the kind that ladies and not school teachers loved.

"Joe was a hero and he acted like a hero at times," said J. Neal Mathews, Beaver Falls High principal. "He was never very popular with some of the teachers."

"Anything Joe did," recalled Tom Krzmienski, "he

did well. He was always a winner. And he always had the girls hanging around."

By now the college football scouts were starting to hang around Beaver Falls, too. Word of Namath's skills had spread to all corners of the country. And the more Joe played, the more he impressed the talent hunters.

Against Ambridge High, considered to be the best team in the Valley, Namath was injured early in the game and spent most of the first half on the bench. In his absence, the Tigers' attack faltered. Then, just before the half ended, Joe returned to the action. And, hero he was, he immediately threw a long touchdown pass to Krzmienski, seconds before intermission.

At halftime, Namath sat in the locker room with an aching shoulder, suffered when Ambridge tacklers had fallen on his arm and driven him from the game in the opening moments.

"Shoulder okay?" Coach Bruno asked him.

Joe nodded.

"Atta boy," Bruno said, and patted him gently on the shoulder.

Namath felt pain shoot through his shoulder when the coach touched him there, but said nothing. He wanted to play football.

He played the second half—if not with his customary brilliance, at least with enough skill to lead Beaver Falls to a 25-13 victory against one of the strongest high school teams in the nation. Ambridge would not lose another game that season. And if Namath did not look as sharp as he had earlier in the season (3 completions in 15 passes), there was a good reason: he'd played with a separated shoulder.

The doctors were amazed at what they discovered.

"You mean, you played football with this?" they asked, probing the shoulder.

Joe said he had.

"Well, son," they told him, "that's the last of football you'll see for this season."

Joe protested. But the doctors stood firm.

"Definitely not. There's just no way of playing football with a shoulder like you have," they told him.

The doctors didn't know Joe Namath's determination.

He went to the team's next pratice in street clothes. With him was his father. Both of them were gloomy; Joe had tears in his eyes.

"Doctors say he can't play," John Namath said. "But the kid wants to."

Larry Bruno looked at the hunched figure of his star player. Bruno had been a small-college star at Geneva College—good enough to play in the East-West Shrine game in 1946. He knew what the doctors didn't: that when a man wanted to play badly enough, sticks and stones and broken bones couldn't stop him. One look at Joe Namath told Bruno that here was a kid who'd do anything to play.

"Cheer up, Joe," he said. "You've got a game to play this week."

Namath looked up in disbelief.

"That's right, son," said Bruno. "We're going to work something out to get you on that football field."

What Bruno did was to send Namath to an orthopedic doctor.

"The doctor fixed him up," Bruno recalled. "He told Joe that with proper rest and a well-taped shoulder, he could play again."

Namath played. A week later against undefeated Butler, all Joe Willie did with a bum shoulder was to complete 11 of 18 passes for 131 yards and two touchdowns. And he did not shy away from contact: he ran for a touchdown, too. Beaver Falls won, 26-6.

Against Farrell High's touted pass defense, Joe was just as good. He completed 13 of 21 passes in a 33-18 Beaver Falls victory. And against Aliquippa, he had his best game of the season. He completed 13 of 17 passes for 232 yards and three touchdowns in a 34-7 victory.

But it was in the next game—Ellwood City—that Namath got his greatest satisfaction. Never mind that Joe Willie hit 12 of 20 passes for 224 yards. More important was the fact that Beaver Falls won 26-0 to clinch its first WPIAL championship in 32 years.

A guy like Joe Willie didn't intend to waste such a splendid occasion. He went downtown with Beaver Fall partisans to celebrate the event. It turned into quite a celebration. As Bill Ross, the school's athletic director remembered: "Joe climbed on the roof of the Sahli Chevrolet building on Seventh Avenue and shinnied up the flag pole. He wanted to tie an orange balloon on the top, advertising Beaver Falls' championship. Well, a crowd started to gather and the police were called and Joe, as usual, got in a helluva mess."

But it was straightened out in plenty of time for the season's finale against New Brighton—a traditional rivalry called the "Little Mud Jug" game. Namath completed 9 of 16 passes for 175 yards. And Beaver Falls completed an undefeated season with a 40-6 victory.

For the season, game-by-game reports gave Namath 85 completions in 146 passes for 1,564 yards and 12 touchdown passes. But Joe's skill as a quarterback was not limited to passing the football. In crucial moments, he'd been a nifty runner, too. He'd run for six touchdowns in '60. And for real aficionados of quarterbacks, there were few schoolboys who could handle a football more slickly than Joe Willie. Four times during the course of a season, Beaver Falls had touchdowns called back because officials had been fooled by Namath's sleight of hand and mistakenly had whistled the play dead for a runner not even carrying the ball. In one game, a veteran official warned his junior partner about Namath's deftness at handling a football, and then blew a quick whistle himself!

It was no wonder that football recruiters came streaming into Beaver Falls after the championship season. "It was almost funny," said Bruno. "We'd have one scout leaving my office, another one crowding in, and a third waiting at the door. A fourth would be looking over game films and a fifth would be checking grades." In all, fifty-two major football schools expressed interest in Namath, but he did not commit himself.

He didn't have time to. Joe played basketball, too. As a senior, the whole first team was from the Lower End, and Namath was the only white boy on it. At 6' 1", he could dunk the ball and dribble and shoot it. Late in the season he and Benny Singleton were the team's leading scorers with 14-point-plus averages. Then came the game against Farrell High, the state's basketball power.

Farrell couldn't miss the basket that night, and things got so bad that Beaver Falls coach Nat Lippe couldn't bear it any longer and ordered both Namath and Singleton to the bench. Angered, Joe and Benny stalked off the court. The coach could do nothing but suspend both of them.

Though he didn't finish the season, he made an impression on basketball people. "Don't worry about your boy playing college football," a coach told John Namath. "If anything happens, he can always get a scholarship for basketball."

But people were offering Joe Willie more than

scholarships. In the baseball season, the major league scouts came around talking money to him. And no wonder! Joe could play any position but catcher. As an outfielder for Beaver Falls, he led the team to a WPIAL championship in '61 hitting, running and throwing with enough skill to draw offers of bonus money.

"When those baseball scouts were watching me," Namath said, "I could pick 'em out. A lot of 'em chew tobacco and they have a heavy tan and wear a hat. Also when you see somebody you never saw before talking to the coach, he's usually a scout. But that never bothered me. I just went out and played my game."

Joe found it exciting to be offered money, and when the Kansas City A's mentioned a $15,000 bonus, the kid from the Lower End was tempted. But John Namath was determined to see that his son got an education. None of his boys had ended up in the steel mills, and Papa Namath didn't want Joe there either if he failed in baseball.

After Kansas City offered Joe $15,000, his father asked him, "And what are you going to do with that kind of money?"

"Well, Dad," said Joe, "I was looking at those new Oldsmobile Jet-85s . . ."

And right there is where John Namath gave Joe a bit of fatherly advice. It didn't take much talking: deep down, Joe Namath wanted to go to college, too.

The question was: where?

3. 'Bama Calls

Bear Bryant is the most fantastic man I've ever met.—
Joe Namath

JOE Namath did not decide right away which college he would attend. First, he had to visit them. And, from the start, he made it clear that his prerequisites for a college were based on more than football.

"I went to Notre Dame," he remembered, "but I nearly had a heart attack when I found out they didn't have women. They said, 'There's a girls' school just across the lake.' I said, 'Man, I don't *swim* after my women. And I don't want to talk to them on no pay phones.' "

He thought he'd found the proper mix of football and femmes at the University of Maryland, but failed to meet the school's entrance requirement. Said Namath: "You needed 750 and I scored 745, right? They wanted me to take it again, but I said to hell with it."

Maryland head coach Tom Nugent was sad to lose Namath. "I knew I was on to something special the first time I visited him in Beaver Falls," he said. "When I took him out to dinner, while he was still in high school, he ordered bourbon and water."

But Namath figured he'd go instead to Penn State, a haven for co-eds and close enough to his home so that his family and friends could watch him play football. But the prospect of playing against Namath—Penn State was on Maryland's schedule—did not enchant the Terps' football people.

Recalled Nugent: "We didn't want to play against Namath, so one of my assistants who had gone to Georgia called Georgia and suggested they sign Joe. The Georgia man we talked to said they weren't interested in 'Maryland castoffs.' So we called Alabama."

Into the land of cotton went Joe Willie, and he liked what he saw. The climate was warm. The girls were pretty. And then there was Paul Bryant, the man called "Bear" because of the time he'd wrestled a grizzly in an Arkansas theater. Namath met him the summer following his graduation from Beaver Falls High.

"I won't forget it," Namath said. "I was with Clem Gryska, the assistant coach, and we walked through the gate to the football field and Coach Bryant was up on his tower about 150 yards down a cinder track. I'd never seen anything like it—Red and White and Blue teams, and the injured in Yellow and Green and Orange teams. Coach Bryant was in a baseball cap with an amplified megaphone. I was 900 miles from home and I wondered what four years like this was gonna be.

"I remember I had longish hair and I was wearing a silvered blue-straw hat with a dark blue band around it and a little pearl on the side and I had a toothpick in my mouth. When we got to the tower, the other coach shouted up to Coach Bryant and he hollered down to me, 'C'mon up.' So I climbed up, and in four years I saw only one other person up there and he was an old high school coach from Texas.

"I think Coach Bryant talked to me for about thirty minutes and that was the first time I ran across the Southern accent. He had such a low pitched voice I could hardly understand him."

He understood enough: the Bear wanted him to play football for Alabama. As Namath later perceived, Bryant didn't make it a habit of inviting people up to the tower from which he studied the team's practices. But Joe Willie was an exception.

The Bear wasn't used to having natural athletes at his school. His specialty was in shaping teams from scraggly lads with an inordinate amount of desire. He did it by demanding that they submit to the kind of physical regimen that would make the ordinary lad buckle.

The boys who stuck it out with Bryant didn't buckle when it counted—on the field. The Bear's teams were always quick and fierce, and they never let up. Late in the game, they would be hitting as aggressively as they had at the opening whistle.

Bryant was a tough, purposeful man. In 1954, his first year at Texas A&M, preseason training camp in Junction, Texas, was aimed at discovering which players were Bear Bryant's kind of men. Complacency had set in among Aggie football players and Bryant was determined to change old attitudes. In the blazing Texas heat, Junction became a concentration camp.

Players moaned and grumbled, and some of them packed their bags and left the camp. Soon word of Bryant's inferno got back to the big city football towns, and before long the Houston *Post* dispatched writer Mickey Herskowitz to Junction to check reports of dissension in the ranks.

Said Bryant to the writer: "Son, I want you to tell your boss that if there isn't any dissension now there's damn sure going to be some—and I'm going to be causing it."

He meant what he said. As a Bryant assistant later recalled: "We took two buses down to Junction, 55 boys. We came back in one bus with 29, but those 29 boys were the making of a team that had a 7-2-1 record a year later, and didn't lose a game [9-0-1] in 1956."

What Bryant communicated in his Dixie drawl to Namath was simple enough: he was a winner. And despite Joe's spirited ways, he could accept the discipline if it meant winning.

Winning was all there was for the Bear. As he had said at a banquet after losing to Santa Clara in the 1950 Orange Bowl: "I'm a win man myself. I don't go for place or show so if you will excuse me. . . ." And he left the banquet.

He demanded that things be done right. At Texas A&M, he'd hauled running back John David Crow out of the shower and shouted, "Okay, let's do it again, only right!"

On his wall was a sign that read: "Winning is not everything, but it sure beats anything that comes in second."

Bryant lived by that credo. As Namath recalled after his college career: "He drove us. He expected the best of us. I remember one Saturday, we lost a game and he called a meeting for 4:30 Sunday morning . . . all hands

. . . and he was right. Four-thirty in the morning! Man, he made losing the worst thing in the world."

So Namath went to Alabama, and immediately wished he hadn't. He couldn't get used to the southerners, and for sure they couldn't get used to him. Joe Willie looked, talked and thought differently than they did.

Coming from a predominately Negro neighborhood, his attitudes on racial issues were bound to be different from the lily-white opinions held by his Dixie peers. Racial prejudice was not new to Namath—when he was ten, a woman in a Beaver Falls pizza place had refused to serve a Negro friend of his—but he had not seen it to the extent it existed in Alabama.

"We used to get into debates," Namath said, "and one of my nicknames was 'Nigger.' Hell, I came to understand that. They were raised a different way than I was, so I didn't try to tell them how to live."

At the same time, he didn't care for being cast as the outsider. It got so that the natives resented him for the threat he represented as a frosh star to the varsity quarterback, an Alabama boy named Jack Hurlbut. In football-mad Tuscaloosa, where the University was located, such things were taken seriously.

The gibes about the way he looked and the way he talked bothered Joe. He hadn't gone to college to feel like a misfit. So when the Baltimore Orioles offered him a $50,000 bonus to quit school and sign with them, Joe Willie gave it serious consideration.

But the people in the football department weren't about to lose Namath. They sat down and talked things out with him. And, eventually, the kid from Beaver Falls changed his mind about leaving Alabama.

"There were fifty-five of us freshmen when I first went to Alabama," Namath said. "Eleven of us stayed.

Accommodations weren't the best, but Coach Bryant told us all that would be changed. We'd have the best."

Life at Alabama soon became easier to take, especially after Paul W. Bryant Hall, the athletic dormitory, opened in 1963. Built like a small Roman Gardens, the place housed 130 athletes—100 football players, 20 basketball players and—as writer Gary Cartwright said—"ten assorted heretics."

People called it the Alabama Hilton—and rightly so. For a college dorm, it was a pleasure palace, just the kind of place a dead-end kid like Namath could appreciate. "He [Bryant] gave us a dorm with wall-to-wall carpeting, maid service, color TVs and phones in our rooms. You went down to the dining room, ordered a steak and told them how you wanted it fixed, and they fixed it. We had powder rooms for our dates and guest rooms for our parents. We had silk jackets for traveling."

On the football field, however, life was more primitive —as Namath discovered in spring drills prior to his first varsity football season. "On the field," Joe recalled, "the motto was: Kill or be killed. He wanted you to put out 110 percent and if you didn't, you were out, that's all. I *worked* for that man. I even played *defense;* would you believe it?"

Bryant shaped his men on and off the field. "He taught us to behave," Namath said. "If he walked up to a boy in the dining hall, for instance, and that boy didn't stand up while he was talking to him, he'd chew him out good and proper. He'd say, 'Listen, boy, when someone walks up to you like this, you stand up and you say *yes sir* and *no sir* and don't you forget it.' He said he wanted us to be able to handle ourselves anywhere, to know we were as good as any other man alive."

The Bear made sure his players knew how good they were. "Once we were playing away from home," Namath said, "and when we got into the airport the team buses weren't there. Coach Bryant ordered cabs. 'My boys are the best football players in the country,' he said. 'I don't want them standing around.' When a coach like Bryant tells you you're the best, you believe it, you go out and play like it. That's why his 180-pounders can whip hell out of 250-pounders."

And that was why a flip guy like Namath could play for the tough-minded Bryant: as a football player, he wanted to be the best. And he could respect the Bear's way of doing things. The Alabama coach, in turn, found that Namath was everything people had said he was as a quarterback. By the end of spring drills, it was obvious that Joe Namath would be the Crimson Tide's starting quarterback in '62, his sophomore year.

Curiously enough, Namath's first varsity game was against Georgia, the school that had rejected him as a "Maryland castoff." Joe proved what a mistaken notion that was. He threw 10 completions in 14 passes for 179 yards and three touchdowns, and ran for 36 more yards in a 35-0 victory.

Even the most Dixie-hearted southerner couldn't help but take to Namath after that. Joe Willie helped ensure his place in their esteem on the autumnal Saturdays to follow. Once Alabama football fans saw that Namath was a winner, regional differences quickly were forgotten.

And Namath was a winner for sure. He threw for two touchdowns and ran for another in a 46-0 win over Tulane, and then completed 7 of 13 passes for 142 yards and two touchdowns in a 17-7 victory over Vanderbilt.

Namath and Alabama kept winning. Houston. Ten-

nessee. Tulsa. Mississippi State. Miami. All lost to
Alabama, now the top ranking team in the nation. In
Tuscaloosa, it was said that Beaver Falls was just a
suburb of Alabama.

Then came the game against Georgia Tech . . . and
the season's biggest disappointment. The strategy was
for Namath to rev up the conservative attack with more
passing—to counteract a defense that had based its
game plan on stopping the running game.

It wasn't a bad idea, but Namath couldn't make it
work. His passing arm just didn't have the magic it had
had in previous games. In fact, Georgia Tech intercepted an early pass thrown by Namath and went on
to score a touchdown for a 7-0 lead.

Alabama came back in the fourth quarter when a
Tech punt backfired and gave Alabama the ball on the
opposition's 9. From there, the Crimson Tide drove in
for the touchdown, and forced Bryant to make a
crucial decision.

The score was 7-6, and Alabama had the option of
trying for one or two points after touchdown. In effect,
the Bear was given the choice of accepting a tie—a
kicked extra point rarely failed—or gambling for victory. "There was no question," said Bryant later. "We
were supposed to be the best team in the nation. When
you're the best, you got to play like it."

The gamble was honorable but it failed. Alabama was
behind 7-6, and there wasn't much time left, only
enough for Namath to get a final chance to salvage the
victory. He almost did it.

He drove the Alabama team steadily down the field
until it had advanced to Georgia Tech's 14. That was
close enough for a field goal, but Namath wanted to
make it even easier for the kicker. On his next play, he
made a daring call and passed the ball, just as Unitas

had passed near the goal line in the Colts' winning drive in the famous sudden death game in '58.

When newsmen asked Unitas why he had risked an interception when the obvious stratagem would have been to run the ball, Johnny U. said, "You don't get intercepted when you know what you're doing."

Like Unitas, Namath knew what he was doing, but he just didn't have the pro's good fortune that afternoon. The ball was thrown away from the Tech defender, but the Alabama receiver bobbled the ball in such a way that it was deflected right into the foe's hands for an interception that finished the Crimson Tide for the afternoon and ruined any chance of an undefeated season.

It was a tough game for Namath. He had completed only 9 of 31 passes for 98 yards, and had blown a golden opportunity to win the game in the final moments.

But Bryant didn't intend to let his team stay down. Alabama had one more regular-season game against Auburn—and the Bear didn't want to see his boys suffering the aftereffects of a Tech loss.

"There's no use talking a long while about those guys," Bryant told the team. "There's no way in the world they can beat you. Hell, they're all wearing Thom McAn shoes, you're all wearing alligators. How the hell you going to lose to a bunch of guys wearing Thom McAn's?"

The implication was clear. Alabama players had class, and now the Bear was asking them to show their class and forget the Tech loss and go out there and knock the stuffings out of Auburn. That is exactly what Namath and his teammates did. Joe threw two touchdown passes, and Alabama won 38-0.

For Namath—the lone loss notwithstanding—it had

been a promising beginning, made more so by his acceptance of Bryant's discipline. On the field, he'd become an extension of his coach's mind, and the Bear marveled at the way the sophomore could handle game situations with so much skill. In particular Bryant admired the way Namath made the team's concern more important than his own. In the Auburn game, Joe Willie had had a chance to break a university seasonal total offense record set by Harry Gilmer in 1945, but had refused to gamble for the yardage that would have given him the record. Rather, he had played Bryant's style of defensive football even if it caused him to lose a chance at the record. It was the kind of sacrifice the Bear could not forget.

But Namath could not forget the blot on the season—the loss to Georgia Tech. Even though he'd completed 76 of 146 passes for 1,192 yards and 12 touchdowns, he still felt responsible for the Tide's only loss. He looked forward to the Orange Bowl game against Oklahoma as a chance to make amends for that game.

Before a capacity Orange Bowl crowd that included President John F. Kennedy, Namath went to work early in the game. On the second Alabama series of plays, he drove the team to the Oklahoma 25, from where he arched a touchdown pass to Richard Williams.

Then Bryant's cat-quick defenders did their share. Two successive Sooner drives were snuffed near the goal line when Alabama tacklers hit Oklahoma fullback Jim Grisham so hard that he fumbled both times. In the second quarter, the 'Bama defense continued applying the pressure. Alabama punter, Cotton Clark, kicked the ball out on the Sooner 8, and the defense drove Oklahoma back to its 4-yard line.

From there, Joe Don Looney punted the ball to Billy Piper, who ran the ball back to the Oklahoma 34.

Now Namath took over. He threw to Williamson again for 23 yards at the Oklahoma 13 and, two plays later, Cotton Clark ran for the touchdown. Alabama 14, Oklahoma 0.

It was a fitting climax for Joe Namath. He threw 9 completions in 17 passes for 86 yards and a touchdown and gained 24 yards running. Alabama won 17-0 and now everybody knew Joe Namath's name.

Well, almost everybody. For in the Alabama dressing room afterwards, a photographer was taking a photo of Bryant when he happened to get the kid quarterback in the same shot.

"What's your name, kid?" he asked bluntly.

"Joe Namath," Bryant replied for him.

"How do you spell it, kid?"

"N-A-M-A-T-H!" Bryant said, in an insulting tone. "J-O-E N-A-M-A-T-H, and I don't think you'll have to ask next year."

For the moment, celebrity was unimportant to Namath. Alabama had won, and the season was over. That meant it was time for celebrating. Again, Joe Willie managed to get in trouble.

This time it occurred when he went to a Miami racetrack and decided to bet the horses. He was prevented from wagering because he was under 21, a situation so absurd to him that he said, "What a rule. I never heard of anyone going to the track and not betting."

Back at Alabama, with its Scarlett O'Hara belles, Joe could have plenty of post-season fun without getting into trouble. He'd settled into the campus life in his own fashion, appearing from time to time in a rakish beret, dark glasses and a zoot suit.

But whether it was in the Soup Shop, a cafeteria where students linger over coffee and donuts, or in one of Tuscaloosa's few night spots, invariably Joe was with a campus beauty.

When it happened he opted not to be in the company of ladies, he'd end up at a cafeteria table filled with athletes. Invariably, good-natured insults would be exchanged.

"Joe, didn't you flunk that ROTC, man?"

"No, man, I knocked hell out them exams. It was them itchy uniforms got me."

"Hey, Joe's had a hard time of it since kindergarten."

"That sandpile's no snap course, man. Better believe it."

"There's no snap courses for you, baby."

Actually, Namath was no slouch in the classroom. As an industrial arts major, he never had troubles with his grades. But for laughs, Joe didn't mind playing dumb.

On the football field, however, he knew his stuff. In his junior year, he opened the season against Georgia by completing 6 of 14 passes for 118 yards and a touchdown in a 32-7 victory. When he led the Tide to victories over Tulane and Vanderbilt, football fever was high in Tuscaloosa. Florida changed all that.

The underdog Florida team took advantage of a misplayed Alabama punt, and returned it to the Tide 28. When the 'Bama defenders resisted, Florida kicked a field goal to take a 3-0 lead. Namath couldn't strike back. His passing was off. He ended up completing 10 of 25 passes for 104 yards and a touchdown, but couldn't come up with the big play late in the game. Florida won 10-6.

Namath came back from adversity. Tennessee (11 of 18 passes for 141 yards and three touchdowns) . . . Houston (13 of 21 passes for 127 yards and two touchdowns) and Mississippi State (10 of 16 passes for 142 yards and a touchdown): all three teams lost to Alabama.

Georgia Tech was next. Bryant's strategy was to play ball control football. Namath passed only three times that afternoon—he completed one for 11 yards—but Joe had his best running game of the season. He carried the ball 13 times for 53 yards and a touchdown. His play selection so befuddled the Tech defenses that Bryant refused to interfere with his quarterback's management of the game. Alabama won 27-11.

The thrill of avenging the '62 Tech defeat may have caused a letdown the next week against Auburn. For Namath was off in his passing—he completed 4 of 17 passes for 43 yards—and Alabama lost 10-8. That was only the beginning of his troubles.

Bryant had gotten reports that Namath had broken training rules by drinking. When he confronted Joe Willie with these allegations, the quarterback confessed to the truth of them, refusing however to implicate others who'd been with him on the binge. It was only months later that Bryant found out that Joe had taken the blame by himself.

There was nothing the Bear could do; he had to suspend Joe. He did, saying, "Namath has been suspended from the team for the rest of the season, including the Sugar Bowl, for an infraction of training rules this past weekend. Joe has indicated to me he will remain in school and concentrate on his studies. He will be allowed to remain on scholarship.

"There is certainly a chance that Joe will come back, but it definitely won't be this season. It all depends on Joe. I believe he's a good boy. He made a mistake, but if he is the kind of person I think he is, he'll prove worthy of another opportunity."

For Namath it was the end of a disappointing season.

Though he had completed 63 of 128 passes for 765 yards and seven touchdowns, rushed for a net total of 201 yards and accumulated a total of 966 yards in Alabama's first nine games, he had failed twice during the season to give the team his best performance. As a result, Alabama had lost twice.

Nothing got to Namath more than losing, not even the fact that his suspension cost him a chance to join Harry Gilmer as Alabama's only two-time 1,000-yard performers.

He did not contest Bryant's decision. Years later, as a pro, he would tell writers, "The Bear was 100 percent right. No, 110 percent." All that was left to Joe was to move from the new athletic dormitory into a men's residence hall on another part of the campus. And prove to Bryant he deserved another chance.

Certainly, Bryant realized that Namath's life style was a bit more eccentric than that of most other boys he coached. He knew that Joe's origins had made him a kind of hell-bent-for-leather social creature. Namath was more impulsive than most of the young men who'd played under him. Before a game that season, the band had struck up a lively tune, and Namath—before 60,000 people—began twisting on the 50-yard line.

Bryant's tolerance was wide-ranging—even Namath would concede that. "I had a goatee after my junior year at Alabama," he said. "Before you went home you had to say goodbye to Coach Bryant and I had to go see him. It's true I had been ducking him because of the goatee, but I had to face him. When I walked in, he said, 'What the hell you got there?' And I said, 'It's a goatee, Coach.' And he said, 'What you got it on for, boy?' And I told him, 'Because I like it.' He said, 'Oh, all right,' and he never said another word about it, but I was scared to death. I had it off by the time I returned for football camp."

He made it to football camp for his senior year. Bryant had lifted the suspension. Namath was a new man for the opportunity. "Before," center George McCullough said, "Joe used to do his job and expect everyone else to do theirs. This year he's after everybody all the way. You can see the team pick up when he comes in."

Namath sparked Alabama right from the season's opening whistle. Against Georgia, he completed 16 passes in 21 attempts for 167 yards and scored three touchdowns on runs of 8, 1 and 5 yards. In all, Namath had a total of 222 yards offense—11 yards short of the school record set by halfback Bobby Marlow in 1951. It was plenty good enough for Joe: Alabama won 31-3.

He kept throwing the ball with good results in the next two ballgames. He completed 10 of 20 passes for 123 yards and two touchdowns in a 33-6 victory over Tulane, and then completed 13 of 23 passes for 141 yards and two touchdowns in a 24-0 shutout over Vanderbilt. It looked as if he were heading for his greatest year at Alabama.

In preparing for the game against North Carolina State, Namath decided not to wrap tape around his lightweight lowcut football shoes. There'd been too much commentary to the effect that Joe did it to look flashy.

Actually the tape served to give his ankles support. When he did not tape them, he would play without the protection he needed. It cost him. For late in the first half against North Carolina State—after he'd completed 7 of 8 passes for 52 yards—he rolled out to his right and started to cut back to his left when his knee collapsed. Alabama won 21-0, but Namath did not play the rest of the game.

For the duration of the season, Namath's knee ached and required intermittent treatment to tap excess fluids from it. Joe Willie played in Alabama's victories over Tennessee and Florida, but not with his customary élan. The trouble was the pain in his knees. It just did not permit Namath to do the things on the football field he wanted to do.

It became so bad for him that Bryant was forced to keep him on the bench in the Tide's 23-6 victory over Mississippi State. And he planned to play him as little as possible against Georgia Tech. But when the undefeated 'Bama club couldn't generate an attack in the first half, Bear looked down the bench at his quarterback and said, "How you feeling?"

Joe indicated he was ready to play.

"All right," Bryant said. "Get in there, and get us moving."

Namath did as he was ordered. On third down from the Georgia Tech 49, he threw to flanker David Ray who ran with the ball all the way to the 1. From there, fullback Steve Bowman went in for the touchdown. Alabama took a 7-0 lead.

Later in the game, Alabama had the ball again at the Tech 49. And again Namath came up with the big play. This time he threw to flanker Ray Ogden down the middle for 46 yards and a first down at the 3. Two plays later, he hit David Ray for the touchdown. In all that afternoon, the hobbling Namath completed 4 of 8 passes for 104 yards and a touchdown. Alabama stayed undefeated, winning 24-7.

'Bama finished the season by beating Auburn behind Namath's 6-for-9 passing performance—good for 76 yards, a touchdown and a perfect season. The victory earned the Crimson Tide the rank of number one team in the nation, and a chance to play in the Orange Bowl against fifth-ranked Texas. Namath finished the season with 64 completions in 100 passes for 757 yards and six touchdowns.

Now there was plenty of time for him to rest his aching knees. But it didn't seem to help. Several days before the Orange Bowl game, Namath's knee gave way while he was doing a routine handoff in a warmup at Miami Stadium. He was rushed to the dressing room where the knee was immediately placed in ice.

"We don't know how serious it is, but this is something that I was afraid of," said Bryant. "If we don't have Namath our chances will be hurt."

Namath, wincing in the dressing room, said, "I intend to play. I will be all right."

Said Bryant: "As of now, Steve Sloan [the No. 2 Alabama quarterback] is my starting quarterback."

Sloan did start, but he couldn't get the Alabama offense going. In Namath's absence, Texas rolled to a 14-0 lead by the second quarter.

Once again, Bryant looked down the bench and ordered Namath into action. Joe Willie's knee was taped, he wore soccer shoes to prevent his cleats from gripping the earth. He was playing with a ripped cartilage in his knee, and everytime he had to throw he could feel the pain.

But he threw the ball anyhow. From the Alabama 13, he completed 6 passes for 81 yards, the final one being to end Wayne Trimble for 7 yards and a touchdown. Texas 14, Alabama 7. Just like that, the kid from Beaver Falls had shown that the Crimson Tide was very definitely in the ball game.

It was the usually reliable defense that put Namath into a bigger hole. Late in the first half, Alabama blocked a punt but fumbled the ball back to Texas on the same play. On a subsequent play, a holding penalty downfield gave Texas the ball on the Alabama 13. From there, the Longhorns drove in for a touchdown by Ernie Koy to make the score 21-7 at the half.

But Namath wasn't finished. Far from it. He put the football into the air early in the second half—and with good results. He hit his receivers three times to advance the football to the Texas 20. Then he dropped back and hit end Ray Perkins for 20 yards and a touchdown. Texas' lead was now only 21-14.

And Alabama was still moving. Namath drove the team 30 yards to the Texas 16. Place kicker David Ray took over at that point and booted a field goal to narrow the margin to 21-17.

Texas couldn't stop Namath. Said Longhorn coach Darrell Royal: "We tried all sorts of defenses against him. We tried to rush him, but it didn't work. He'd hit us then with those quick ones. We tried dropping back. He still hit. He's fantastic about anticipating the route his receiver runs. The second the receiver cuts, boom, Namath lets go."

In the fourth quarter, Alabama intercepted a Texas pass at the Longhorn 34. Namath passed to Ogden for 17 yards, to Bowman for a first down at the 6. On the next play, Bowman drove closer to the goal line. He carried twice more, but did not score. It was fourth down at the one-yard line. The big play of the game.

"When I came to the line of scrimmage right before the play," said Namath, "I thought I saw an opening. I thought I could make it."

He almost did. When he plunged into the Texas line, there was a moment of uncertainty on the part of the officials. "One official said it was a touchdown," said an Alabama player afterwards. "Two others came running over and said, 'Are you sure?' And they talked him out of it."

Said Namath: "I knew I was over on the sneak, but the referee said I wasn't."

For all practical purposes, the game ended there: Texas 21, Alabama 17. There was a final sequence of Alabama plays, but Namath was under a great handicap. He could hardly see. He was slammed down so hard on his first pass play that there was only a vision of blue in his right eye.

Trainer Jim Goosetree sped out and applied a potion to clear up his vision, but it didn't seem to help. Namath overthrew Perkins, underthrew Ray and had his last pass of the day batted aside.

In the final minutes of his final game for Alabama, he sat on the bench swishing water in his mouth and feeling down. When somebody told Joe Willie that he'd be named the game's Most Valuable Player for his record Orange Bowl performance—18 of 37 passes for 255 yards and two touchdowns—Joe said yeah and crumpled the cup and threw it down.

Like Bear Bryant, he was a win man himself.

Still, it had been a memorable college career, and if the disappointment seemed hard to bear, at least there would be many games ahead for him in the pros.

4. The Making of Broadway Joe

"I remember," Joe Namath once said, "when this baseball player [Bob Bailey of Pittsburgh] received a $200,000 bonus. I was a college freshman at the time and I was amazed when I read it in the paper. I couldn't believe it. We talked about it for days around the school."

By Namath's senior year, that kind of money was kid's stuff compared to what pro football teams were offering Joe. The NFL St. Louis Cardinals and the AFL New York Jets both were prepared to pay Namath roughly $400,000 to play pro football.

Namath's inclination was to play in New York. Like sailors drawn to Circe's song, Namath was attracted to the bright lights and good times of the big city. Of course, the money that Jet owner David A. (Sonny)

Werblin was offering—New York writer Dick Young detailed it as $427,000—didn't compromise the Jets' chance of landing him. St. Louis made a good bid, too, but it wasn't quite to Joe's liking.

"They had it laid out wrong, like I had to do a radio show for part of my salary," Joe said. "I couldn't believe that. I said, man, I'm just a football player, and what I make will be for football only."

So, before the Orange Bowl game of 1965, Namath advised Werblin he would play for the Jets, which did not assure Sonny quite enough. "I called Bear Bryant about it," Werblin recalled. "He said, do you have his word? I said yes, but I'd like to have something on paper; I'd feel better about it. Bear said, you don't need it. If he gave you his word, you don't need the paper."

He didn't. Namath signed shortly after the Orange Bowl, a contract so highly publicized that Bob Hope quipped, "Joe Namath's the only quarterback in history who'll play in a business suit."

The money was no laughing matter to other established pros, who had missed out on the bonus riches that the presence of the new league, the AFL, caused.

"If that kid is worth $400,000," said Cleveland quarterback Frank Ryan, "I'm worth a million."

"Any bonus baby who has that much money before he starts," said Green Bay tackle Dave (Hawg) Hanner, "is not going to be willing to pay the price you have to pay in pro football."

Namath bristled at that kind of talk. "You don't play four years under Coach Bryant without paying the price," he said. "You give every gut you have or you don't play. Ask anybody who ever played for Coach Bryant and they'll tell you the same thing."

One man who had played for Bryant was Ray Abruzzese, and he knew that Namath could pay the price. "I never thought he'd play in the Orange Bowl," Abruzzese said. "He was limping real bad on the leg and he was in real pain. I don't know how he went out there."

Bryant himself said, "This is not only the greatest athlete I have ever coached. He's the greatest I have ever seen. He is big and strong. He is quick as a cat— with lightening hands. He is perfectly coordinated, and he has a trigger mind. He should be a great pro."

Namath, always candid, agreed: "You can forget all about my injury, the pressure on me, everything. Throw them all out, I tell you, because I am going to make it.

"I can throw the ball all the way out to my belt buckle and still hold on to it. On a fake that good, a defensive back—I don't care who he is—has got to take a step in toward the receiver. That's one reason why I tell people that, as far as the mechanics—passing, handing off and so on—are concerned, I think I'm ready for the pros."

Prelimary reports indictated he was also ready for Manhattan's social whirl. After Werblin's 19-year-old son, Hubbard, accompanied Namath for a night on the town, he reported back: "That Joe's a real swinger, Dad. We double-dated at a discotheque on 58th Street, and you should have seen him on the dance floor. He can do it all—monkey, swim, Freddy, mouse. He's the wildest."

Namath could afford to be the wildest—with his sudden riches. His living quarters rivalled Hugh Hefner's for elegance. The apartment, located on Manhattan's fashionable upper East Side, cost Namath $500 a month rent and was decorated at a cost of $25,000. The outstanding feature of this exotic indoor Xanadu was an oval, satin-sheeted bed. *The New York Times* found it chic enough to feature on its fashion page, remarking on the Siberian snow-leopard throw pillows, the cheetah-skin bench, the pair of brown suede sofas and the wall-to-wall white llama rug, six inches thick. For get-togethers and parties, there was a black-leather bar, fully stocked.

To be sure, there were plenty of get-togethers and parties, social affairs differentiated by Namath. "A get-together," said Joe, "is when the guys come over to eat steaks and play cards. A party is when there are girls. Of course, a get-together can turn into a party."

After the limited attractions of Tuscaloosa, New York night life was just what Joe needed. He jumped into it with gusto.

And why not? "Look, how do I know I'll be here next year?" he said. "How do you know you'll be here?"

When Namath went about town, nothing was planned. Joe just let things happen. "I don't date so much as I just, you know, run into something," he said. Whether it was at P. J. Clarke's, the *Pussycat,* or Mr. Laffs, Namath managed to encounter women. He was seen with movie star Mamie Van Doren, dancer Carol Doda and various other ladies, mostly blondes.

"A girl with brown hair is all right," he said. "So is one with black hair. But blondes, they come first."

Where other athletes were furtive about their night prowling for the sake of image, Namath wasn't. "Me, . . ." smiled Namath, lighting a cigarette, "my only weaknesses are clothes and women."

After a boyhood of deprivation, he indulged his hedonism. "This apartment," he said about his pad, "was not meant to appeal to women. It was meant to appeal to me."

Such candor was typical of Namath. In word and deed, he had no pretensions. There was, for instance, his intermittent yearning for a lipful of snuff. Joe Willie took his pleasure where he could, even at genteel places like the Waldorf-Astoria—he simply spat the juices into one of the Waldorf's teacups.

He was just as up-front about his ladies. In response to a female interviewer's question on why he hadn't gotten married, Namath said, "I guess I've been too busy. Back when I was at college . . . well, playing for Paul Bryant is like being in the Army . . . you work all the time. You work, eat, sleep, live with other players, all in the same dorm. You travel back and forth to games. There's too much happening to get attached to one person. Same thing here in New York, only more so. I don't think I've had more than two or three dates, like for dinner or something formal, since I got here. I just bump into girls on the fly and from that you don't fall in love."

To the same interviewer, Ann Borowik, Namath conceded he'd fallen for certain girls before. "I went steady with a girl in high school and after I went away to Alabama we wrote, but when I went home again I found out I just didn't have any feeling for her anymore. There've been some girls since. If I didn't like girls, I'd be abnormal, right?"

The only thing abnormal about Namath was his right knee. It required surgical treatment. The trouble was that the medial meniscus, one of the two pads of cartilage that lie between the thigh and shinbone, was torn and rolled back in a tight wad. This accounted for Namath's inability to straighten his leg completely. The crumpled cartilage had the same effect a newspaper stuck between a door would have—it prevented total flexibility.

The Jets' surgeon, orthopedist James A. Nicholas, followed the accepted medical procedure for disabilities of Namath's sort, and cut out the meniscus. This did not leave Joe with a cavity in the knee for, by natural processes, air and body fluids filled the space and compensated for the lost cartilage.

At the same time, Nicholas found that a ligament in the knee had been pulled and stretched. To tighten it, he doubled it back on itself and pleated it with sutures.

In all ways, the operation was considered successful, but it was only the beginning for Namath. For now he had to undergo the painful and strenuous process of rehabilitating the knee. A graduated series of exercises was calculated to have the knee ready for training camp.

In July the knee was ready. Namath was ready. And the Jets were ready and waiting—for knee and Namath. New York's fullback, Matt Snell, said, "A lot of guys are just sitting back and waiting. They don't say anything now because, if Namath does come through, they don't want to make fools of themselves. On the other hand, the other day in the locker room, one guy said: 'I hear he's ready to meet the guys in this league.' Then somebody else said: 'He'll meet 'em, and they'll all want a piece of that $400,000.' "

The pressure didn't bother Namath. He remained confident of his ability, even when he had difficulties adjusting to the cumbersome knee brace he had to wear.

"Joe," Coach Weeb Ewbank said to him the first day of training camp, "you're throwing off your back foot and you're not getting enough follow-through."

"Don't worry, coach," Joe Willie said. "Once I get loosened up, I'll hit all those s.o.b.s."

Off the field, Namath was plenty loose. The first Saturday-off the team had, Joe took two other rookies in his convertible for blind dates with three girls he had met in downtown Peekskill, New York, the site of the Jets' training camp. In short time, the rookie had a reputation among the players as a Lothario, a reputation that practical jokers on the team sought to exploit.

One day, Jet flanker Don Maynard knocked at Joe's door.

"Yeah," said Joe.

"Telephone call," said Maynard.

"Who is it?"

"Girl."

"Oh!"

"Yeah, she said she's your cousin."

Namath went to the phone and a while later was seen slipping into nifty sports clothes and wheeling his Lincoln Continental toward New York.

Unbeknownst to Namath, he was trailed by teammates in another car. They saw him park his car and stand on a corner and wait.

After a while, the players drove by.

"Need a lift, Joe?" the players asked.

"No," he said. "I'm waiting for somebody."

"See you then."

And they drove off, laughing hysterically. It had all been a gag. The players had gotten a Peekskill girl to call and make a phony date.

Namath laughed it off. More crucial things concerned him, in particular his fight to win the quarterback job for the Jets. The competition was plenty tough—including veteran Mike Taliaferro and another rookie, $200,000 bonus baby John Huarte of Notre Dame.

The money the Jets had spent on Namath meant nothing to Ewbank. "The guy who puts the ball in the end zone, that's my quarterback," Ewbank said. "The rest doesn't mean a thing to me. I'm not running a bank, I'm running a football team."

The three quarterbacks were rivals and yet they were teammates who shared the same room. In front of outsiders, they played it for laughs.

"Last night," Huarte told a newsman, smiling, "Joe tried to knife me in my sleep. I woke up just in time."

"I wish they'd give the veteran more respect," Taliaferro said.

"Yeah, John," said Namath. "You were supposed to buy us an air-conditioner."

"Why me?" Huarte asked.

"Because you're outvoted, two to one, right Mike?"

"Sure," Taliaferro said, "I bought the TV set." Motioning to the 12-inch portable TV that faces his bed, Taliaferro said, poker-faced, "The TV set was my bonus."

For all the intramural levity, each man was dead-serious about winning the quarterback job. The routine problems a rookie has were made more complex in Namath's case. The knee brace he was ordered to wear hindered his mobility, and plagued the balance he was accustomed to before throwing. At first, he had a hard time hitting his receivers.

That was only part of the challenge he had to meet. He had to learn to get rid of the ball quicker. At Alabama, he had had the agility to elude onrushing linemen. But with his knee, he no longer could depend on footwork. For the Jets, he was required to drop back deeper into the protective pocket and pass the ball before the fierce pro-style pass rush devoured him. That meant he had to set up to throw as quickly as possible.

It also meant that he had to be able to decipher the complex defensive maneuvers that pro teams attempt in breaking down an attack. For only if he could interpret the rushing choreographies of the opposition could he anticipate his own receivers.

This was no easy chore. It required experience. As a result, Namath's intentions did not always coincide with his receivers'. "At first," said split end George Sauer, "he couldn't anticipate the way we'd cut. The ball was always there early or late."

Or with too much acceleration. "That's right," recalled Don Maynard. "Joe'd put a lot of mustard on those passes rookie season. He'd knock us over on short patterns. He had to learn to ease up on the football."

There were other pressures, too, not the least of which was the threat of military induction. Namath failed his physical examination, but because of his fame he was forced to re-test several times. Public clamor eventually forced the Department of the Army to prepare a statement on Namath's 4-F classification, part of which read:

It may seem illogical that an individual who is physically active in civilian athletics should be found unfit for military service. When playing professional football, it must be presumed that Mr. Namath does so with the counsel and preparation of doctors and trainers. He is closely watched and professional assistance is close at hand at every game and practice session. In the military service, these conditions would not necessarily be present. In Vietnam, for example, the life and safety of his comrades could depend on Namath performing his duties under extremely adverse conditions.

Physical standards, as applied by the Armed Forces, represent our best professional knowledge and we apply them equitably to all persons. It would be discriminatory to take action in Mr. Namath's case that would differ from that taken in the case of any other individual. . . .

Despite the army's absolution, public opinion had

Namath down as unpatriotic. "How can I win, man?" he asked. "If I say I'm glad, I'm a traitor, and if I say I'm sorry, I'm a fool."

But however much the public damned Namath, they wanted to see him play football. Jet season ticket sales rose from 11,000 to 35,000 on the strength of Joe Willie's presence on the roster.

There were, however, no guarantees that the kid from Beaver Falls would be the quarterback. He was going to have to prove he was good enough to start. From his showing in the first exhibition game against the Boston Patriots, it looked as if he might be.

In that game, Namath completed 9 of 19 passes for 106 yards and two touchdowns in a 23-6 victory. It was a good debut, and Namath should have been feeling proud afterwards. But he did not show it in the dressing room.

"The big thing is we won," he said. "I don't care how I did. We won. That's why we play football. To win."

On the bus leaving the high school football stadium where the game had been played, Namath did show his pleasure.

"Thirty minute stop for a beer," he yelled.

"Yeah," one of the other players said. "Namath's buying."

"If we stop," Namath quipped, "I'll buy. Gladly."

The bus did not stop.

Nor did Namath. Two weeks later in Allentown, Pennsylvania, not far from Beaver Falls, the Jets played the Patriots in an exhibition again on Friday, August 13, a date that left Namath uneasy.

"I thought it was . . . say . . . odd for us to be playing a game on Friday the 13th when I first heard it a month ago," he said. "When they told me I would start, I thought about it again. I shouldn't have worried though."

The Patriots were the ones to worry. Namath completed 4 of 6 passes for 80 yards and a touchdown. His touchdown pass was a pretty 60-yard play to Maynard. It floated like a butterfly and Maynard pulled it in on his fingertips at the 27 and raced to the end zone untouched. "A couple of plays before, Don said he thought he could beat his man long," Namath said. "No, I didn't just lay it out there for him to catch up to. I aim all my passes."

The only unpleasant moment for Namath was when Patriot linebacker Mike Dukes landed on him after the whistle. Joe Willie looked ready to throw the ball at Dukes, but didn't. "Me pick on a big guy like that?" he said, smiling. "I jumped up just to make sure the ref called it. I survived and we got 15 yards for it."

However, not everything turned Namath's way in the pre-season grind. In other games, he made mistakes common to inexperienced quarterbacks, the kind of mistakes that the veteran Taliaferro didn't make. As the season drew near, it was clear that Namath was still learning.

For Ewbank, the problem was whether he should let Namath learn under regular-season game pressures or not. Ewbank decided not to start Joe Willie merely for the sake of satisfying the curiosity of the football world and Werblin, too.

Werblin was outspokenly in favor of Namath's being the regular quarterback, but little Weeb—a man some people mockingly called "The Jolly Green Midget"—stood up to his boss.

"He's not ready yet," said Ewbank.

"But when?" asked Werblin.

"Not for a while. He's got things to learn."

So when Namath's rookie season (1965) opened, Joe did his learning on the bench in Houston, Texas.

He sat there for the entire Oiler game and manned the field telephone from which he conveyed information from the coaching staff high above the stadium to Ewbank and Taliaferro on the playing field.

It was a frustrating experience for Namath. Not since Beaver Falls days had he been deemed inferior to another quarterback. What made it more frustrating for him was the way the Jets played that afternoon. Starting quarterback Taliaferro completed only 4 of 22 passes for 58 yards, and the Jets lost 27-21.

Namath could do nothing but wait for his chance to play. He got it the next week against the Kansas City Chiefs in Shea Stadium. Again Taliaferro couldn't hit his passes and when the crowd of 53,658—at that time an AFL attendance record—began shouting for Namath, Ewbank ordered him to action in the second quarter.

Namath trotted onto the field in his light weight white Puma shoes—white for superstition's sake after what had happened to his knee in the North Carolina State game. His first pass was to Maynard for 18 yards and a first down at the New York 48.

The crowd roared, anticipating more $400,000-kind of miracles. There were no miracles right away. Namath threw to Snell for a loss of 4, then threw incomplete to Maynard and Snell.

But in the fourth quarter, Namath started hitting. With the score 14-3, Joe Willie threw to Bake Turner in the open, forcing a Chief defender to interfere with the pass for a 36-yard penalty. Then Namath let fly with a 36-yard touchdown pass to Maynard, the first of his pro career. Kansas City 14, New York 10.

In all, Namath completed 11 of 23 passes for 121 yards and a touchdown, but he couldn't get another touchdown. Despite a promising start by Joe, New York lost 14-10.

Ewbank figured the situation would improve. "The timing between receiver and thrower," he said, "is not the best. Our pass game's been hampered by sorting out the three quarterbacks we've used. A receiver has to get used to one quarterback to be most effective."

On the strength of his performance against Kansas City, Namath became the starter against Buffalo. And he did something that Taliaferro hadn't: he moved the team. Joe completed 19 of 40 passes for 287 yards and two touchdowns, and prompted Bill's coach Lou Saban to say, "I thought Namath did an excellent job. He's an oustanding player."

It was easy for Saban to be so gracious about the foe: the Bills had won 33-21. On the other hand, Namath didn't feel he could afford to be so laudatory about the afternoon's work. "Being a rookie is murder," he said. "There's so much to learn. Did you see the perfect timing [Buffalo quarterback Jack] Kemp has? That's what this game is . . . perfect timing, perfect timing."

Namath did not perfect his timing. In fact, it grew worse under game conditions. He threw for no touchdowns against Denver and was 5 for 21 against Oakland when Ewbank sent in Taliaferro to salvage a 24-24 tie.

"I've been watching Joe throw," said Ewbank. "From favoring that bad knee he's lost his footwork and started throwing with just his arm. We've got to overcome those bad habits."

Namath did not get a chance to overcome those bad habits right away. Instead, Ewbank gave him a chance to think about what he was doing. Joe Willie returned to the bench.

In the Jets' next two games against San Diego (34-9 loss) and Denver (45-10 victory), Namath was used only in the closing moments. For the prideful rookie, it was the low moment of the season, made worse by the prospect of further bench duty, implicit in which was his failure to make it as a big-leaguer.

Not that Namath ever doubted he had the ability. From the day he had told Ewbank not to worry, he'd hit the s.o.b.s, Joe Willie never lacked for confidence. "If you're quarterback, always handling the ball, you got to have confidence," he said.

His gloom was not a product of shattered ego so much as frustration. Namath had anticipated there would be difficulties. It was part of the process of a quarterback's growth. Even his paragon of quarterbacks, the great Johnny U., had had his bad moments as a rookie. But Unitas had gotten the chance to make his mistakes, and learn by them. He had gotten playing time. It was the lack of opportunity that bugged Joe Willie.

But Ewbank's responsibilities were not solely to Namath. His job was to do what was best for the team, even if it meant sacrificing the immediate growth of his quarterback. Ewbank had not lost faith in Namath, but he owed it to Taliaferro to start him until he played himself out of the job.

That happened in the Jets' next game against Kansas City. Ewbank ordered the ball to be thrown short, but Taliaferro kept throwing the ball deep and—worse—incomplete. Finally in the second half, Weeb sent in Namath to replace the veteran. It was the last time Joe Willie would be a substitute.

When Namath went into the game, the Jets were trailing the Chiefs. By the time the final half had ended, Joe Willie had completed 7 of 16 passes for 81 yards and a touchdown, and New York had a come-from-behind victory, 13-10, the first Jet win on the road in 13 games.

"You never know about a young quarterback," Kansas City Coach Hank Stram said of Namath. "Either he gets you into a lot of trouble or he gets the job done. He is a great young one."

He looked even better against the Boston Patriots the next week. As a starter again, Namath controlled the game in the manner of a seasoned pro, particularly in the team's final drive.

There were more than nine minutes remaining in the game, with the Jets leading 27-20. New York needed to score again, but also to waste as much time as possible doing it. And that's just what Namath did.

He brought the Jets down the field, alternately passing and running the football, always conscious of the ticking clock. Slowly, steadily, New York advanced the football, driving the Boston defense to distraction with the methodical destruction of time, Boston's only resource for victory at this point. It was no use, the Patriots could not stop Namath—he brought the Jets into field goal position. Jim Turner kicked the three-pointer, and the game ended. New York 30, Boston 20. It was a very professional performance.

After the game, a man in Tuscaloosa, Alabama, picked up the phone and called Namath.

"How's it going, Joe?" the man asked.

"Fine, sir," Namath said.

"Just called to tell you that you became a pro quarterback today. You looked darned good down the stretch."

"Thanks, Coach Bryant. Thanks a lot."

Indeed, Namath had become a pro quarterback. He showed that against the Houston Oilers the next week— his finest game as a rookie. Joe completed 17 of 26 passes for 221 yards, four touchdowns and a 41-14 victory—the New Yorkers' fourth straight victory of the season.

The modest winning streak made believers of the Jet players. "The big thing about him," said Maynard, "is his coolness under stress. I don't think you can do anything to make this guy lose his poise.

"In addition, he knows his football. The coaches set up a weekly game plan, but Joe calls our plays. Not many rookies could do it."

It was not just Namath's savvy at quarterback that won the respect of the players. "He's taken quite a beating but the leg has held up," said Maynard. "Some big lineman will bust through to flatten him. But Joe bounces back and continues to do his job. If his knee hurts, he never lets anybody know about it."

From Ewbank, he won the highest kind of praise, comparison with Unitas, whom Weeb had coached at Baltimore: "They work hard, like to throw, get rid of the ball quickly, and are competitors. Joe also has shown he can take it his first year. He's been hit and hit hard. And I've never seen any young man handle the two-minutes-to-go offense better than Joe."

But Namath was by no means the complete quarterback yet. He continued to look good the rest of the season—he ended up with 164 completions in 340 attempts for 2,220 yards and 18 touchdowns—but he showed one serious flaw. He threw too many interceptions.

There were several reasons for the interceptions. For one thing, Namath did not have enough experience to know when it was better just to throw the ball away rather than risk an interception. He had too much pride in his ability to drill the ball past defenders. Secondly, he was only beginning to accustom himself to the stylized moves of his receivers. Maynard, for instance, often departed from the pattern he was assigned to run and a quarterback was forced to adjust quickly or look foolish when the ball was thrown where Maynard was not. Sauer, on the other hand, ran his patterns perfectly. It required great precision to get the pass to him just as he made the break for the ball. And finally, Shea Stadium—the home field of the Jets—had tricky wind currents that often caused a football to stray from the direction in which it was thrown.

All these factors produced the rash of interceptions Namath threw toward the end of his rookie season— nine in his last four games. But that had no effect on the minds of the football experts, who named Namath as AFL Rookie of the Year, and the only rookie for the All-Star team that would play against AFL champion Buffalo.

It was in the All-Star game that Namath provided the perfect finishing touch to his rookie season. He came off the bench in the second half, threw two touchdown passes to San Diego's Lance Alworth and prompted one pro football man, Houston's John Breen, to exclaim, "Look at him, he's picking them to pieces."

The way Namath threw the football, the All-Stars got a come-from-behind victory and Joe Willie got the game's Most Valuable Player award.

He also won this tribute from Houston Oiler flanker Charley Hennigan, an All-Star teammate for the day: "He throws a beautiful ball. You don't have to stay there and say, 'c'mon, ball.' You know it's there. But the thing I like best about him is the way he is in the huddle. He's no rookie there. I've been in huddles with signal callers and I've been in huddles with quarterbacks. Namath's a quarterback."

It was the kind of talk that made Namath wish he could start another football season the next week.

5. The Pain Behind the Game

DESPITE the false starts, Joe Namath had proved he belonged in professional football during his rookie season of 1965 with the Jets. The Jets' management was convinced of this, the players were convinced, and the fans and writers sensed that Namath was not very far from leading the team to an American Football League championship. Perhaps the person least convinced that he belonged was Joe Namath himself.

Perhaps that explains his return to the University of Alabama campus in Tuscaloosa during the spring of 1966. Ostensibly he returned to the scene of his college stardom to help Bear Bryant tutor the quarterbacks during spring football practice. But the fact was that Namath would have attempted to swim the English Channel at the behest of Coach Bryant, such was the

reverence in which Namath held his Alabama mentor.
It was this reverence which sublimated Namath's tolerance of Weeb Ewbank, the Jet's coach, during his first
season with the team.

Sam DeLuca, an offensive guard for the Jets for
three seasons before an exhibition game injury in 1967
forced him into retirement, recalls Namath's attitude
toward Bryant and Ewbank: "It always seemed to me
that Namath was comparing Ewbank to Bryant and
that Bryant always came out ahead. Joe would say,
'Bryant would have done it another way' to us in the
locker room and even on the field and for all I know he
even said it to Weeb himself. You could sense that Joe
didn't have the greatest respect for Ewbank but that he
worshiped Bear Bryant."

His brief return to the Alabama campus did give
Namath an opportunity to escape the New York clime
and the growing concern about his knee. "I think," he
told the Jets before embarking south, "I'm going to
need another operation."

Joe had played all during the 1965 season with a
brace on his knee to prevent it from collapsing under
him. The brace reduced his mobility to a minimum and
he asked the Jets' management around midseason if he
could have an operation which would clear up the
problem and eliminate the need for the brace. The
Jets consulted one surgeon who told them: "There *is*
an operation that will do this, but it is very risky.
Namath can end up either with a perfect knee or without a knee to stand on." The Jets refused to give
Namath another operation.

In the spring following his rookie campaign, Namath's knee pained him constantly and he again asked
the Jets to allow him to have another operation. But
again a doctor advised against it. "You don't need

another operation," he told Joe. "You certainly don't have a perfect knee and you probably never will. But as long as you can play well enough to be named Rookie of the Year, there's no point risking further surgery."

In the sunny atmosphere of his old college campus, Namath was able to put the anxieties over his knee out of his mind. He found relaxation amid the casual banter and give-and-take with the Alabama players out for spring practice. "Some of the players asked me about my poor start," Namath recalled, "and I admitted that I was making a lot of mistakes. Like throwing off my back foot and not getting enough follow-through. Then I was missing a lot of wide open receivers. After a while I was able to recognize a defense and I'd figure, 'Well, this play will work against that defense.' Then it wouldn't work and I'd feel bad. I was real down for a while.

"Then I had that good five minutes against San Diego and I thought I could handle the job."

Whether Bryant helped Namath erase some of his self-doubts, or whether the time spent away from the hectic New York life also played a part in lifting Joe's attitude, when Namath arrived at the Jets' training camp at Peekskill in July of 1966, his teammates were ready to accept him as their leader. In fact, when Namath arose at the team's first get-acquainted meeting of the camp at the Peekskill Military Academy, and introduced himself as "Joe Namath, quarterback" and a teammate quipped, "Joe who?" the room exploded with laughter.

Off the field, Namath was further establishing himself as a man about New York nightspots. He settled into a penthouse apartment some 20 stories above Manhattan's East Side with roomate Ray Abruzzese, an old friend from the days at Alabama who spent two seasons in the Jet livery. After training camp sessions, Namath and Abruzzese would tool back into New York where, on warm evenings they could be seen on the prowl in East Side discotheques. Invariably, their companions were pretty airline stewardesses and models. Namath and Abruzzese would take turns livening up the places they frequented with their blend of humor and cornball. One example:

Joe: "Say, Ray, what was Billy The Kid's middle name?"

Ray: "I don't know, Joe. What was it?"

Joe: "The."

On the field, Joe was a different individual from the high-priced rookie who had reported to the 1965 Jets' camp. "A lot has changed," Joe confided to a writer. "Now I've got the job for as long as I can hold it. Now I want to be part of a championship club. And one day the Jets will be champions."

A championship for New York seemed far off after an exhibition game against Houston that summer of 1966. On one play that afternoon, Matt Snell, New York's running back, fumbled a handoff from Namath and the ball was picked up by Ernie Ladd, the Oilers' mountainous 300-pound tackle, who started running toward the New York goal. At that point Don Floyd, Houston's 245-pound defensive end hurled himself into Namath to block him from the play. Namath toppled to the turf and lay motionless for several seconds until the Jets' coaches and team physican Dr. James Nicholas reached his side.

Namath was convinced of the worst. "It's gone, I tell you," he moaned in pain. "My knee feels like it's just hanging there by a thread." But Dr. Nicholas, after inspecting the damaged area with his fingers, told Joe:

"I know you're scared to death but it looks like just a minor sprain behind the knee. It has nothing to do with the surgery."

However, the injury was serious enough to sideline Namath for most of the pre-season, and while he sat idle, another problem developed. This time it involved Joe's left knee—his "good" one. A tendon in the knee had become inflamed, leaving a jabbing and constantly throbbing sensation in the area. The inflammation had developed, the doctors explained, during the previous season when Joe, in an attempt to favor his damaged right knee, had effected a compensatory running motion.

As Namath put it: "If I sit in a car or a plane for a half hour with my knees bent, it starts hurting. But heck, I figure anybody can put up with a little pain. You don't think about it during the game. It's only afterward that it hurts."

"Psychologically, it was a tremendous feat for him to go out there for a game with those old man's knees," said DeLuca, the guard who then was the Jets' offensive captain. "It's tough enough out there when you can go 100 percent. When you can go only 50 percent you've got to be thinking: How will I do? Will I get hurt because I can't go all-out? It has to affect you. But I'll say this for Joe, I admire him for it. Not once did I ever hear him complain about the pain or use his knees as an excuse when he had a bad day."

Late in the 1966 training season, when Namath was able to participate briefly in practice sessions, the pain in his knees was so intense that Joe hobbled around, unsuccessfully trying to hide the grimace of pain which constantly marred his face. The team medical staff shot his knees full of cortisone and bound both knees in braces and tapes. By the end of the training camp season, Joe was ready for regular league play.

One man not willing to risk the Jets' star quarterback immediately to the rigors of combat was New York coach Ewbank. The Jets' first game was against the brand new expansion team, the Miami Dolphins, in the Orange Bowl. Mike Taliaferro started the game at quarterback for New York, but when the Jets left the field with only a 9-0 halftime lead over the expansion team, Ewbank decided to insert Namath into the lineup for the second half.

On a sun-baked Miami gridiron before 34,102 fans, Namath directed the Jets to a touchdown and a field goal in the third quarter, following a pair of interceptions by Johnny Sample. With 10 points in the third quarter for a 19-0 lead going into the final quarter, the heavily-favored Jets appeared to have victory well in their grasp. But the determined Dolphins struck for two touchdowns in the last 15 minutes of play. Midway through the period, Miami cornerback Pete Jaquess intercepted a Namath pass and ran 27 yards for a touchdown that reduced the Jets' lead to 19-14.

The Dolphins stopped the Jets after the ensuing kickoff and got the ball back with three minutes to go and a final opportunity to pull off an upset victory. But with the ball on the Miami 26, Dolphin quarterback Rick Norton threw into the flat where the ball was intercepted by Namath's roomate Abruzzese and the Jets then ran out the clock.

Statistically, the Miami game was not a brilliant one for Namath, especially against a new team. Joe completed eight of his 18 passes for 100 yards. And when the Jets left the field, they left with doubts as to whether Namath's knees would be sound enough for the sterner competition they would face in the weeks ahead from the more established AFL teams.

Namath, his knees paining him, also had doubts, but

he had his own methods of putting them aside. On one midweek evening before the second game, which would send the Jets against the awesome line of the Houston Oilers, Namath gathered with friends at *Dudes 'n Dolls,* a Third Avenue drinking spot he favored. "Man, my knees are completely fouled up," he announced when he arrived around midnight in a natty blue sports jacket with French cuffs.

Joe walked directly to a favorite booth in the back of the place and stretched out his injured right leg. As he nibbled at a plate of spareribs with his fingers, he took in the pulsating rhythms being pounded out by the Outcasts, the musical combo appearing at *Dudes 'n Dolls* for the evening. The conversation at the table was mostly football. "You know, I couldn't play anything but quarterback," Joe offered. "As far as I'm concerned, the knees are ruined for life. I just got to make adjustments from week to week. That's all. But worried? I ain't worried about a thing."

Suddenly, as if the glass in front of him felt insulted by Namath's words, Joe's drink tipped over on the table. An embarrassed silence hung in the air for a moment or two until Al Hassan, an old friend of Syrian decent from the Pennsylvania days, shouted at a waitress, "Here, sombody clean this up. Somebody get Joe another drink."

Having regained his composure by now, Joe bellowed at the waitress, "Hey, Miss America!" A young waitress in a skimpy black costume and high heels approached nervously. "The name's Barbara."

"Hey, get a load of that," Joe said. "She's Barbara. Get me another drink, Barbara. Get us another tablecloth. Give us another everything."

The waitress left and Joe slouched down in the leather seat and began puffing on a cigarette. He took in two demure brunettes who were seated at the next table. When the Outcasts broke into electronic song, Joe rose, ambled behind the chair of the prettier brunette, touched her shoulder lightly and said, "Hey, wanna dance?"

The girl walked stiffly to the dance floor, and once there began gyrating wildly. Joe snapped his fingers, shrugged his shoulders and turned slowly. All eyes in the place were on him, not the girl. "Go, Joe baby, go!" Al Hassan yelled. Then, softer to an observer, Hassan revealed, "Joe's like this every time he's hurt. You know, like he hasn't got a care in the world. Happy. I've seen him hurt before. Listen, no one in New York knows the real Joe Namath because there are three Joe Namaths. There's the Joe Namath from Beaver Falls, the one from Alabama and the New York Joe."

The New York Joe walked off the dance floor in his slouchy, arm-swinging stride. Leaning over beside the girl, he ducked his head and said shyly, "Now, Debbie, if you would just write your address and phone number down here on my card, please."

It started to rain and Namath and his friends sat waiting for it to let up. To cut momentary boredom, Joe showed the girl named Debbie, by now seated at the table with him, a trick with a lit cigarette. "Look at this, baby, you never saw this done before." He placed the lit end of the cigarette firmly against the index finger of his throwing hand, then flipped it up into his mouth. He repeated the trick two more times, seeming to burn himself on the last attempt. "Aw come on, let's beat this joint."

In the rain-splattered taxi which Namath commandeered at a red light outside the *Dudes 'n Dolls,* the driver grumbled about the few blocks he was forced to cover. "Don't get all bothered, buddy," Joe told the driver. "Just take it easy, baby. We just live day to day."

"Oh yeah. I been driving twelve hours straight. I want to go home."

"I work hard myself. Live a little. Don't worry so much."

The new spot for the evening was the *Pussycat* on East 49th Street. "Man, look at those two chicks over at the bar," Namath exclaimed, casting his eyes at two leggy girls with platinum wigs. "A little bit I'd go over and talk to 'em." But he said nothing to similar looking girls who sat at the table next to his.

Later, Al Hassan spoke about the Beaver Falls Joe. "I remember once we bought our way into a poker game, Joe and I. We only had six bucks between us, all the money we had saved one summer. And we lost. What times we had! I remember we were in a clothing store once, and Joe was cutting up the way he does, you know. This woman says 'What a loudmouth! What an obnoxious boy!' Know what? Right now she's telling everybody how well she knew Joe back in the old days, what good friends they were. That's Beaver Falls for you."

Back again at *Dudes 'n Dolls*, Joe was talking one minute to a blonde in a Huck Finn hat, huge sunglasses, and bell-bottomed trousers, and the next he had disappeared into the rain. "Joe is the greatest athlete in the world," Al Hassan was saying. "If his knees hold up no one will ever be able to catch him. Hey where is he? He was going to take me over to *Jilly's*. Hey, he wouldn't run out on me like that. He'll be back. I know he will."

Torrents of rain pelted against the front window of *Dudes 'n Dolls*, obscuring the view of nearly deserted Third Avenue to the late stayers. But Beaver Falls Joe had split.

If Namath didn't seem overly concerned about the game against the Oilers, the Houston team was presenting some real problems for many other Jets. The biggest problem was a 6′ 9″, 315-pound tackle named Ernie Ladd, who, when not decapitating opposing players on the football field, was wiping out the rest of the pro wrestling population during the offseason. A couple of days before the game, Namath sat in Toots Shor's world renowned midtown establishment and discussed the Houston game with the equally renowned proprietor.

Toots, who has a gimpy leg and needs a cane, chided Joe, "You creepy bum. You need a cane, too. Ladd is going to squash you Sunday."

"Not me," laughed Namath over a martini. "I'm lean, mean, mobile, agile, and hostile."

On Sunday the sky was picture-book blue, a hint of autumn pervaded the air and Shea Stadium was filled with 54,681 screaming fans. When the lineups were announced, the Oilers' Don Floyd, who had been involved in Namath's pre-season injury, was vehemently booed. Then Number 99 for the Oilers, monstrous Ernie Ladd, charged out on the field like a bull. He looked surprisingly boyish.

Then came the Jets in dramatic order, with Namath finally trotting on in low-cut white shoes, his face concealed in the white plastic helment. At midfield, he did a neat showman's turn and hustled to the sidelines. The Jets would receive the opening kickoff and Joe talked to Coach Ewbank for a final few seconds as the receiving team fielded the Houston kickoff.

The first few series of downs for both teams passed routinely. Neither side could mount a sustained attack. George Blanda kicked a field goal to put Houston ahead 3-0, but Joe was taking cognizance of one arresting development in front of him.

"The protection I was getting in the line was fantastic," he echoed over and over after the game. "They kept the big guys out and I had all the time I needed to operate." Sam DeLuca and Dave Herman, the New York guards, scoffed at their extreme height and weight disadvantages and successfully throttled the towering Ladd and his defensive tackle partner, Pat Holmes, a 6′ 5″, 265-pounder.

"The key play was to pass to George Sauer," Namath said after the game. "I looked at four guys before I saw George—and still had time to throw to him."

The play was a 67-yard touchdown pass on which Namath made perfect connections with Sauer, who took the ball over his shoulder in full gallop. The play had started like any other with Joe taking the handoff and skipping back into the pocket while thundering hoofs swept past him. But it started the Jets on the road to scoring the most points in a game in their seven-year history.

Early in the second quarter, Namath began a hobbling rollout to the right, then fired a screen pass to fullback Matt Snell in the left flat for a 25-yard touchdown. Before the first half was over, Namath threw his third touchdown pass of the game, 13 yards to tight end Pete Lammons.

With a bulging 21-6 halftime lead, Namath couldn't have been blamed for trying to play it safe against the tough Houston team and not risk being done in by the Oiler defense. But in the third quarter, there was Namath backpedaling time and again and letting fly to his receivers with the Oiler defenders charging in on him all the while. The play that finally convinced Houston that they would not beat the Jets this day occurred early in the third quarter. Namath got the center snap on the New York 45 and moved back into the pocket. But on one of the rare occasions all afternoon when the Jets allowed him to penetrate, Ernie Ladd came charging through at Joe. A moan submerged the entire stadium. Somehow Namath spotted flanker Don Maynard on the goal line and put the ball squarely in his arms for a 55-yard touchdown. The play provoked this comment from one shocked Houston lineman:

"Nobody gets rid of a ball faster than Joe Namath. You can blitz on him and you'll always know where to find him because he can't run. But you got to get to him awfully quick or the ball is gone.

On the 55-yard play to Maynard, two Houston linemen hit Namath chest high. "We looked at the movies of that play," said Maynard a few days later, "and you wouldn't believe it. Those two guys smacked into Joe and ate him up. You could see Joe's elbow actually resting on one guy's shoulder as he threw. Yet Joe got rid of that ball with a flick of his wrist, and he threw the darn thing to me for a touchdown."

Later in the third quarter Namath and Maynard got together again for a 37-yard touchdown. It was Joe's fifth scoring toss of the game, and when he left the game after three quarters with the Jets leading 38-13, the stands thundered with cheers. Taliaferro quarterbacked New York to two more scores in the final period to close out a devastating 52-13 triumph, the most satisfying the Jets had ever achieved. The Oilers had been taught a lesson for their pre-season mauling of Namath.

In the flush of victory, Namath could afford to be expansive regarding the condition in which his knee had survived the game. "It held up very well," he observed, "mainly because I didn't get hit." But the right knee hurt and the left knee began to flare painfully, a jabbing pain that endured for hours and left a throbbing ache. The pain was caused by an inflamed tendon. The doctors put braces and tape on the knees and shot them full of cortisone. This was becoming customary fare for Namath. At practice, when he wasn't getting the shots, Joe hobbled around, grimacing like he had shattered glass for kneecaps.

Joe was ready on the third Sunday of the season when the Jets met the Broncos in Denver. The Denver club was one of the poorest in the AFL and New York was heavily favored, particularly because of the ease with which the Jets had dismembered Houston. But Namath got off to a slow start against the Broncos. He completed just six of his first 19 passes and Denver scored on a 67-yard pass play in the second period to leave the field with a 7-0 half-time lead.

Although Namath was becoming accustomed to the battering he was receiving each week from opposing defenders, Joe must have been surprised by the special attention given him by one Bronco defender in particular. "Johnny Bramlett, one of their linebackers, is a buddy of mine," Namath reflected later. "He had me over to dinner the night before the game. His wife cooked an Italian feast, plenty good, too. But the next day Johnny was after me like a tiger, and he'd cuss me when he missed. He wanted to win, man. That's the way it is. I don't think any of our opponents are too interested in my health."

In the second half of the Denver game Joe regained his health. Under orders from Ewbank, Namath abandoned the long passes he had attempted in the first half and switched to a ball-control type of offense. Utilizing his running backs, Namath concentrated on picking up short yardage and saved his passing for third-down situations. The strategy worked perfectly. Six times in the second half, Namath completed third down passes for first downs and kept the ball in the

Jets' hands. Two of those completions led to Jim Turner field goals. Two others helped produce the lone Jet touchdown of the game, scored by Snell on a five-yard pass. After his abysmal start, Namath completed the game with 16 completions in 35 attempts.

Namath emerged from the Denver game as bloodied and bruised as usual, but the Jets were confident that he could go the following Sunday in a crucial clash with the Patriots in Boston. For three quarters of that contest, New York partisans couldn't have been blamed for feeling that the Jets might have been better off if Joe had not been available for the game.

In the face of the Patriots' fierce pass rush, Namath could do nothing for the first 47 minutes as Boston built up a 24-7 bulge. Houston Antwine, one of the Boston tackles, was getting to Namath so frequently through the first three periods that by the final quarter Ewbank had to revise the blocking assignments of the Jets' offensive line. Rather than continue to try to stop Antwine with man-to-man coverage, Ewbank assigned two men to Antwine. He also ordered Namath to fade deeper into the pocket in setting up to pass—as many as 12 yards back—and called for a double-wing offense, in which flankers lined up on both sides. The idea was to force Boston out of its planned defense—and the idea did just that. "The double wing ruined us," explained Boston linebacker Tommy Addison. "With a pinpoint passer like Namath, it's pretty tough to play man-to-man coverage of his receivers. They simply forced us into a defense we didn't want to use."

Mike Holovak, the Patriots' coach, admitted that "after the Jets double-teamed Antwine, Namath picked us apart. The passes he wasn't getting off in the first three quarters he began hitting all over the field." Still, time was in Boston's favor when New York began abandoning its original tactics. The Jets would have to get the ball at least three times and score three times to wrest victory from the Patriots. A sudden switch in offensive tactics by Boston helped the Jets' cause here.

Patriots' quarterback Babe Parilli, who had outshone Namath for more than a half, suddenly stopped passing after one attempt early in the third quarter was intercepted and another fell incomplete. Thereafter, on three successive third down plays when the Patriots could have passed to try to retain possession, Parilli called a running play. All three times it failed.

Given the extra opportunities to fire the football, and capitalizing on Ewbank's decision to install a third wide receiver into the lineup—the second flanker complementing the original flanker and split end—Namath took control of the ballgame. First he hit Bake Turner, the added wide receiver, for 26 yards, then he hit Sauer for 11 yards on his favorite sideline pattern. A Boston defender was penalized for a face mask tackle on Sauer and the ball was advanced to the Boston 10. From there, Namath hit Snell with a quick pass for the touchdown. Twelve minutes and one second remained in the game.

After a punt by the stymied Patriots, the Jets started from their own 44 with a 42-yard Namath bomb to Turner. On the next play, Namath hit tight end Pete Lammons in the end zone for the 12-yard TD. With eight minutes and three seconds to go, New York now trailed only 24-21.

Another Boston punt gave the Jets possession again, and Namath maneuvered his forces into position for another score, but Jim Turner's field goal from 30 yards away went wide to the left.

While their fans jeered from the stands, the Patriots failed to make a first down on their next series and again relinquished possession to New York. Now time was becoming a critical factor. The Jets had time for only one more drive down the field. Using short sideline passes to conserve valuable seconds on the clock, Namath moved his team relentlessly toward the Boston end zone as the taunts from the stands mounted.

A New York victory appeared certain when the Jets reached the Patriots' 15 with less than a minute to play. Boston's defenses and morale were completely shaken. On third down, a confident Namath stood over center and barked signals for what would be a pass into the end zone.

The ball was snapped. But in his eagerness to execute what he hoped would be the game-winning play, Namath fumbled it. Players from both sides dove to the ground in a fight for the loose pigskin. But Namath reached it first, falling on top of it and pressing it to his chest.

The play had lost only two yards. But on fourth down the Jets decided not to gamble. Jim Turner came into the game and kicked a 17-yard field goal from a perfect position in the middle of the field. The clock showed 32 seconds and the score was tied 24-24.

Boston still had time for three plays but failed to produce a first down. On fourth down, the downcast Patriots performed an act that symbolized their fourth-period collapse: they punted. Despite the late fumble, his fourth period heroics had been a masterful clutch showing for Namath. In the last period of play, Joe completed 14 of his 23 passes for 205 yards. In the three previous periods of the game, he had managed 14 completions in 33 attempts for only 133 yards. "The game was dull for the first three quarters," Joe told a reporter after the game. "After that it was fun."

The fun continued when the Jets returned to Shea Stadium the following Sunday to play the San Diego

Chargers, a club feared around the league as a potential champion. Like the Jets, they were undefeated coming in and the largest crowd in AFL history—63,497—squeezed into Shea for the game. With both teams sputtering on offense, New York managed a 10-9 halftime lead, a Namath to Snell 17-yard scoring pass in the first quarter and a second period field goal by Jim Turner offsetting three San Diego field goals by Dick Van Raaphorst.

The third quarter produced no further scoring, as neither Namath nor his San Diego counterparts, Steve Tensi and John Hadl, could get their clubs moving. Early in the fourth quarter, Joe came off the field yelling to Ewbank about a referee's decision, but he cooled quickly. Namath then flared again and yelled at the bench, "OK, defense, we stop them now and next time we go all the way."

The Chargers weren't listening to Namath's exhortations and on the next series they struck for a score, a 67-yard TD bomb from Hadl to Keith Lincoln sending San Diego ahead 16-10. The Chargers picked a most unlikely situation—second down and 42 yards to go—to go for the deep maneuver to their fullback.

But the Jets hit back for 66 yards in five plays to regain the lead. Namath began the rally by locating fullback Bill Mathis on a 44-yard play which carried to the San Diego 22. On a play which went awry, Matt Snell lost seven yards after taking a pitchout, but Namath recovered the ground by hitting George Sauer for 17 yards and a first down on the 12. Then Namath gave the ball twice in a row to Emerson Boozer and the rookie running back streaked to paydirt. Boozer picked up four yards on his first carry, then tore out of a would-be tackler's grasp at the eight and burst across with six minutes and twenty-three seconds remaining.

The Chargers were not through. Hadl drove them down the field and all the way to the New York 30. When the San Diego drive stalled at that point, Van Raaphorst, who had been successful on nine of ten field goal attempts coming into the game, came on to try for a three-pointer. But his boot was deflected in the air by Jets' tackle Paul Rochester and dived dismally into the Shea Stadium turf.

The Jets had only to run out the clock from that point. But the Chargers' defense stiffened, and less than a minute later San Diego had the ball again. This time the Chargers weren't going to be denied. As the partisan New York crowd gazed on in stunned disbelief, Hadl beat the Jets' pass defense twice in a row. Long aerials to Lance Alworth and Gary Garrison swept the Californians to a first down on the New York 14—point blank field goal range. But, incredibly, Van Raaphorst, called on to kick a field goal from the 21, lofted the ball wide to the right with 25 seconds left. This time the Jets ran out the clock, and when the gun sounded they found themselves with a 4-0-1 record and championship visions, just as Namath had predicted.

Although it wasn't a big game for Joe statistically— 11 completions in 22 attempts for 129 yards and the one scoring pass to Snell—nobody could recall seeing Namath leave the field with a bigger grin than after the San Diego game. That night, by way of celebration, Joe emigrated to East 49th Street's *Pussycat* in the company of a go-go dancer named Suzy Storm, Phil Rodgers, the golfer, and none other than John Hadl, who had come close to quarterbacking his Chargers past the Jets only a few hours before. "Football is football," Joe explained to someone who found it unusual that two rivals would crave each other's company, "and fun is fun."

Monday is typically an off day for pro football

players, and Joe used the next day to fly back to Beaver Falls, he said, to see his dog. "Yeh, little Irish-setter pup, he about tore my brother's house up." Did Joe like going back to his hometown, someone asked. "Naw," he replied. Then, "Yeh, I mean. I like to go back and see my family, but I wouldn't go back there to live. I like a different type of atmosphere, more relaxing, where there's water out there, sking, not the steel-mill stacks where the smoke's coming out, and everyone's going to work and coming home from work."

It was certain that no one in Beaver Falls suffered as much at his work as Namath was suffering at his. The simple fact, as the Jets faced a rematch with the Oilers in Houston, was that Joe's knees hurt. The bursitis in the "good" knee, the left, was acting up. The right knee was being drained regularly. Still, with another game against the hated Oilers coming up, Namath needed no more incentive to overlook his pain. Of course, this didn't mean he had to neglect his post-practice outings.

Thursday night found Namath in the company of jockey Bill Hartack, racing columnist Joe Hirsch, who is one of Joe's closest friends, and their dates. "We started at the *Pussycat*," confessed Joe later, "then to the *Copa,* then back to the *Pussycat*. I got in about five." That night he was out late again. "Joe likes the lights, it's part of his personality," Sonny Werblin, the show-business man and Jets' owner, explained. However, Joe's nightly forays around town were soon to ignite a major controversy.

The plane ride to Houston on Saturday for the Sunday afternoon game in Rice University Stadium was relaxed and cheerful. All of the other Jets had arrived in green team blazers. Joe wore a blue blazer. He slept most of the way, clutching a pillow to his chest. When he opened his eyes, a pretty stewardess batted hers several times and smiled, "Why don't you sleep on your big hairy rug?"

At the hotel in Houston there were people calling, "Mr. Namath, message for Mr. Namath." All the Jets were met with the respect reserved for teams that come into a city undefeated. People from the Houston newspapers and television stations pursued various members of the Jets for interviews and tapes. Even right up to game time a TV announcer with a tape recorder in the Jets' locker room was asking Matt Snell to say, five times in a row for some electronic reason: "This is Matt Snell of the New York Jets." That was probably the last time all afternoon that any of the Jets could be sure of who he was.

The pattern of the game was established on the fourth play when New York halfback Bill Mathis fumbled and Houston's Scott Appleton recovered on the 35. George Blanda, the Oilers' ancient quarterback, moved his team slowly but inexorably down the field until John Henry Johnson, another aging veteran, bulled through the entire Jets' defense for a 28-yard touchdown. The Jets got the ball, but a third-down pass to Maynard was broken up and they had to punt. Coming off the field Namath, who had been knocked flat as he passed, said quietly to Maynard, "I was there, Don." The New York flanker nodded; he had been there too, but so had a pass defender. In fact the entire Oiler defense was playing completly unlike the squad that had been massacred 52-13 in the first meeting of the two clubs four weeks earlier. In particular, Ernie Ladd and Pat Holmes, who had been denied entrance into the Jets' backfield in the first game, spent this particular afternoon tossing Namath to the ground time and again like a rag doll.

Instead of throwing five touchdown passes as he had in the earlier game, Namath threw four passes into Houston hands and completed 15 of 36 passes for only 137 yards. On two successive series in the second quarter, Joe was intercepted in the midst of rallies. Meanwhile, Blanda posted a second-period field goal and threw a 42-yard touchdown pass, and with two minutes to go in the half, Houston led 17-0. Weeb Ewbank looked at his bench. "Anyone have anything?" he asked. No one had.

The second half was worse. Joe, who had endured the most severe pass rush the Jets had come up against all season, was intercepted again. In the fourth quarter it was 24-0 and all New York defenses were down. Ernie Ladd, as if to wreak vengeance on Namath personally for the Jets' earlier humiliation of the Oilers, leveled Joe early in the fourth period and Namath got up slowly, working his shoulders. "I thought about staying down," Namath said later, "but I heard them yelling, and I wasn't going to lay there." Mike Taliaferro finished the game at quarterback for the Jets and moved them toward the goal, but they couldn't push the ball across. The game ended 24-0, the first time the Jets had been shut out in 34 games. For Joe, he said, it was the first time since junior high school.

The loss unearthed New York from first place, a position the Jets had held since the beginning of the season. Namath was visibly upset as he sat in front of his locker. Reporters fired one question after another at Namath. One query in particular rankled Joe and he rebelled. The question stemmed from a muttered allegation made moments earlier by one of the Jets' assistant coaches that too many of the players were "drinking and running around." That made Joe angry. It wasn't justified, he said. "This isn't high school."

Then turning on the reporter who had asked the question, Joe exclaimed, "Hell, what are you looking for? Instead of picking on this and picking on that, why don't you write that Houston played a great game out there. Give them credit. They beat us because they were the better team today."

Over in the Houston locker room, Oiler coach Wally Lemm was enjoying himself at the expense of the Jets, this time verbally instead of visually as he had all afternoon. "We changed our defenses entirely for this game," smiled Lemm. "It did seem to make a difference, didn't it?"

On the flight back to New York, Joe tried to forget about the game. But this was a game he wasn't going to be allowed to forget quickly. Among other things, his knees wouldn't let Namath forget. They felt bad. "Just the usual, but it gripes me more and more," Namath was telling a knot of people in the aisle next to his seat on the plane. To ease the pain in his right knee, he had called for an ice pack. Suddenly his good leg was shot through with a cramping pain and Joe grabbed the leg and winced. He stood up to walk it off. As he walked, he grabbed the arm of a magazine writer who was traveling with the Jets, and said, almost plaintively, "I'm so racked up. This is the first time in my life I've thought about quitting football." Five minutes later he was back in his seat laughing again with his companions. Apparently, the pain had become tolerable again.

The next day, Monday, the drinking charges were brought up again. Back in the *Pussycat,* Namath sat and discussed the allegations with friends. "Look," he said, "I'm no hypocrite. I don't hide anything. I like girls. But some people say we were out clowning and drinking too much and that's why we lost. They said we didn't take this game seriously. It's like we pushed the panic button. That's what teed all of us off."

Namath was clearly affected by the accusations made about the Jets' nocturnal habits. His neglected beer turning flat in his hand, Namath flicked the glass with his thumb and said, "Football is responsible for every opportunity I have. I'm not going to put that in jeopardy. I study what I have to do on a football field. I get to bed on time when I'm supposed to. I'm not going to let having a good time affect my physical status. The way some people put it they got me an alcoholic."

His jacket crawled up his neck. "We're going to come back," Namath said. "I hope people don't think this is going to hurt our team. The quicker I forget this, the better I'll feel. It's like trying to let one game carry you the rest of the season. This time last year we hadn't won a game yet. Can you image how we felt then?"

If Namath's listeners couldn't imagine, events of the next few weeks served to rekindle their memory of the 1965 season. It was hardly Joe's fault, but the Sunday after the second Houston game, the Jets contrived to lose to the underdog Oakland Raiders in the final two seconds 24-21. Not only did Namath have one of his best afternoons of the season, pitching 19 complete passes in 32 tries for 372 yards, but he also scored the first two touchdowns of his professional career, exposing his painful legs to more pounding than ever before.

Namath's first touchdown came in the opening period at the end of a 50-yard drive following an interception. A 38-yard strike from Namath to Maynard put the ball on the Oakland four, and three plays later Joe faked a handoff and rolled out to his left, the ball hidden on his hip. By the time the Raiders discovered the fake, Namath was in the end zone. As if he had been there all his life, Joe casually flipped the ball to a spectator in the stands. The Jets led 7-0.

Namath's second score, on a third-down sneak from the one, sent the Jets ahead 14-7 shortly before half-time, after a 31-yard scoring pass by Oakland had evened the score.

There was no scoring in the third quarter, but it ended with Oakland on the Jets' nine-yard line, and in the opening moments of the last period, Oakland tied it up with another touchdown pass. A field goal a few minutes later sent the Raiders ahead for the first time 17-14.

Confidently, Namath came back again with a series of flare and screen passes that sent New York streaking toward the Raiders' end zone again. Joe found Snell for 21 yards, then Maynard for 12, Lammons for seven, and Mathis for 18 more. Three plays later Snell slithered out of the arms of several tacklers and raced 14 yards to the one. On the next down Snell slammed over for the score that made it 21-17.

With five minutes and one second left, Tom Flores engineered a drive that couldn't have worked any better from the Oakland standpoint. Not only did the Raiders march all the way down the field on the strength of Flores' clutch passing, but they also all but consumed the time on the clock. Fullback Hewritt Dixon finally crashed over from the one with two seconds left—and the Jets lost for the second straight time. The score, 24-21.

Frustrated and complaining of a headache and sore legs, Namath still found time to analyze the defeat. Speaking of his own two touchdowns, he pointed out that Ewbank had installed the quarterback option only that week. Ewbank's move was unusual in itself. The

New York coach had always sought to protect his quarterback from risking his knees. "When a quarterback runs," Ewbank often said, "finally he doesn't get up."

For the first time all season, Namath was thrown for a loss, an event he saw both good and bad in. "I was going to throw the ball relatively quick," explained the man whom a Houston lineman claimed got rid of a football faster than anybody else. "I tried to throw it to Snell but a guy was too close to him." So Joe ate the ball for the first time, crumbling before a two-armed rush by Oakland's 250-pound Dan Birdwell, who stopped Namath 17 yards behind the line of scrimmage and pinned Namath to the Shea Stadium turf by sticking his elbows in Joe's face.

On the plus side, learning when to eat the football is part of a quarterback's repertoire. In the loss to Houston, Namath had been criticized for passing with defenders draped all around him and blocking his view downfield. "I shouldn't have gone through with it," he said later. "There's times when I have to learn that going down with the ball is better than throwing it." Being flattened by Oakland's Birdwell proved that Joe was learning.

Oakland's battering of Namath had set the stage for one of pro football's fiercest rivalries. But, by now, Joe was fair game all around the league. This was never reflected better than against Buffalo the following Sunday when the 1966 season virtually ended for the Jets. They went down to defeat for the third straight time, 33-23, before 61,552 supporters at Shea Stadium. One reporter covering the game called it "the worst performance in the Jets' three years in Shea Stadium." Buffalo's savage front four defensive line was the reason. The defense was primed for Namath. "The front four put up $10 apiece," said Tom Sestak, Buffalo's 270-pound defensive tackle, "and the guy who got to Namath the most got it all."

Ron McDole, a 250-pound defensive end, won the Namath sweepstakes. He won it by clobbering Namath for a 15-yard loss in the third quarter. When McDole rose to his feet after the play, he went around shaking his teammates' hands with the enthusiasm of a man who'd just cashed in a big parlay at the racetrack. "We actually got to him just that once," McDole recalled later. "But quite a few times we hit him just as he passed."

This type of harassment by the front four paid off handsomely for the Bills. They intercepted Namath five times, narrowly missing two more. Although Joe passed for 343 yards on 24 completions in 53 attempts, most of this total came in the final period after the Bills had stormed to a 30-3 advantage by the end of three quarters.

Despite his late heroics, during which Namath threw last-period touchdowns to Lammons and Maynard, many in the capacity crowd started for the Shea Stadium exits with eight minutes to go after Joe had been intercepted twice within three minutes. That had never happened before so early and in such volume. And never before had Namath been booed by a home crowd. The booing began in the second period and built as the game wore on until the jeers reached a peak in the final 15 minutes. In the locker room, though visibly shaken by both the Buffalo defensive might and by the fans' taunts, Joe tried to appear casual. "Why make so much out of the booing? It's not going to depress me."

What did depress Joe were the continued accusations that New York was losing because he was concentrating more on his social life than on football. Namath didn't object to writers who wrote stories about his private life as a man about town. He had already shown several reporters around his plush apartment and had been in the company of reporters on several of his nights out. What Namath feared was that the stories might be giving people the wrong idea.

"I go out like anybody else," Joe said. "What difference does it make? I really don't care if the writers follow me around just as long as they write the truth. I do care when it's exaggerated. Half the things written about me have so many things wrong, it's ridiculous.

"When I had the bad leg and was limping," Namath continued, "one guy wrote that I was in Shor's—with no sign of a limp. But the worst one was a guy who interviewed the team dentist about some of the mouthpieces the guys on the team wear during a game, and he asked the dentist if I wore one. The dentist said it's impossible for me to wear one because I'm the quarterback. I have to call the signals so I can't have a mouthpiece in my mouth. So this guy wrote 'Joe's impossible.' Then the dentist told him that players who don't wear them because they don't like them could get used to them if they concentrated on it. You know how that came out? 'If Joe could concentrate more he'd be a much better player.' He should get his facts straightened out."

Sonny Werblin tried to straighten out the facts on Joe's night life. "The things you must consider about Joe," said Werblin, "are that he is twenty-three, single, and doesn't have to be at work till noon. So what if he drops into a night club? As a general rule he brings files home with him from practice. He'll study them in his apartment from five till about eight. Then he'll go to dinner. He likes movies. He may take in a show.

He'll get out about midnight and pop into a night spot for an hour or two. Joe is the kind of guy who knows everyone from some place or another—and everyone knows him."

To escape from all the people he knew and who knew him, Namath left New York for a three-day vacation in Puerto Rico—on doctor's orders. The Jets were not scheduled to play the following Sunday, and Jets' physician Dr. James Nicholas thought a few days rest in the balmy climate would be good for Joe. Dr. Nicholas said Namath had suffered a bruised rib and a strained rib cage against Buffalo, although neither was serious. But his legs had held up well, the physician said. "They came out of this game better than any other this season."

Sadly, Namath's rest could not uplift the Jets' sagging fortunes. A rematch against the Bills in Buffalo turned out to be one of the strangest games of the entire pro football season. Neither side could do anything right, Joe was erratic in his passing, and at the half the scoreboard showed no points for either side. The only scoring in the third quarter was a 43-yard field goal by the Jets' Jim Turner, but in the final period Buffalo scored twice to win the game 14-3. The second touchdown was scored by the Bills' mammoth 297-pound tackle, Jim Dunaway, who blocked another field goal attempt by Turner at the 28 and lumbered all the way to the New York goal 72 yards away. In the dressing room after the game, one jubilant Buffalo player called for "Jim Dunaway for offensive back of the week."

There was no such jubilation in the Jets' dressing room. The whole club had been flat all afternoon in losing its fourth straight and falling further behind Boston, now leading the Eastern Division. Namath, with only eight completions during the first three quar-

ters, had come slightly alive in the closing period with
11 successful attempts in 16 for 136 yards. But he
still couldn't throw for a score. A harried Ewbank got
impatient with the writers. The fans had come to expect
too much of Namath, Ewbank said, because of his
big publicity buildup. "Before he ever held a football
in his hand, they all thought he'd throw a touchdown
on every play in the pros. That's not going to happen.
Just let the kid develop normally," Ewbank pleaded.
"Don't put him on a pedestal and let everybody chop
him down."

Sam DeLuca praised Namath for not blaming his
knees for his poor play. But there were some who
thought Joe should use his knees as an excuse—to stop
playing entirely. "I wish Joey would quit," said Namath's mother, Rose. "I don't want his knees to be
injured anymore. I don't want him becoming crippled."

Mrs. Namath realized, however, that football meant
too much to her son for him to give it up. So she
developed a method to give him her support. "I pray
to one saint when he has the ball," she said, "and I
pray to another saint when the other team has it. Joe
got a kick out of it when I told him. He said I had
an offensive saint and a defensive saint. He's always
making cracks like that, but none of them, I guess, gets
him into trouble. He doesn't mean anything by them.
He's just being funny."

Against the Miami Dolphins, both of Mrs. Namath's
saints must have been working for Joe. The Jets finally
halted their losing streak, beating the expansion team
30-13. First, New York gave the 58,664 Shea Stadium
fans a scare by falling behind 6-0 in the opening period
on two Miami field goals. The booing, which had begun
in the Jets' previous home game against Buffalo, began
to fill the big ballpark again. Then Joe began to pick

apart the Miami defense. With Emerson Boozer running brilliantly and George Sauer latching onto eight passes for 144 yards, the Jets moved ahead, 10-6, by the half and increased their margin to 23-6 by the beginning of the fourth quarter. A Dolphin TD march narrowed the gap to 23-13, but Mark Smolinski, subbing at fullback for the injured Matt Snell, barged across the goal line to cap a 49-yard drive with one minute and forty-nine seconds left to play for the touchdown that made the final score 30-13.

Though Namath failed to throw for a touchdown, his performance was one of his best to that time as a pro. He was successful with 17 of his 30 passes, gaining 236 yards through the air. None of his throws was intercepted.

But the Jets' first victory in five weeks—including the one week when there was no game scheduled —did not trigger the hoped-for change in the team's fortunes. The following Sunday, the Jets hosted the Kansas City Chiefs and had the dubious distinction of allowing their guests to clinch the Western Division title from which they were to advance to the first Super Bowl. With two touchdowns in the decisive third quarter, the Chiefs went on to a 32-24 victory. The two Kansas City scores in the third period gave the Chiefs a 29-10 lead and Namath's touchdown passes of 18 yards to Sauer and seven yards to Smolinski in the last period proved too little too late. Again an erratic first half by Namath had hurt the Jet cause. At intermission, Kansas City had led 16-10, with the Jet scores having come on a three-yard burst by Smolinski and a Jim Turner field goal. Namath finished with 18 completions in 36 tries for 263 yards but the Jets now faced the prospect of dropping under .500

after a 4-0-1 start. After 11 games, their record read five wins, five losses, and a tie.

The prospects for remaining above .500 did not appear good as the Jets prepared for their next game against the Raiders in Oakland. New York hadn't been able to beat the Raiders in Namath's three previous games against them. Most of the Raiders seemed to treat a game against the Jets as their own private war, and Namath in particular was the target of much of the in-fighting.

This time it was no different. The onrushing Oakland front four harassed Joe into five interceptions, one of which was carried into the end zone by linebacker Dan Conners after a 23-yard run early in the fourth quarter and gave the Raiders a seemingly safe 28-20 lead. Only a minute earlier, Tom Flores and Oakland end Art Powell had combined for their second long scoring pass play of the game to wipe out a 20-14 New York lead.

On New York's first scrimmage play following Powell's second touchdown, Namath's attempt to pass was quelled as Oakland's giant mustachioed tackle Ben Davidson swarmed all over Joe. The ball squirted a few yards out of Namath's grasp and Conners swooped it up and went in untouched for the score, giving the Raiders two lightning TD's within 43 seconds.

But Namath wasn't yet through. Thirteen minutes remained in the game, and for 12 of them the Raiders continued to hold the New York quarterback in check by forcing him to throw hurriedly and then spilling him to the turf after his quick release. With five minutes left, Joe took a headlock from Davidson and threw his fourth interception into the arms of Warren Powers at the Jet 25. Behind a devastating block by Davidson,

Powers went into the end zone for another apparent touchdown. Here fate intervened as the officials ruled the ball dead at the point of interception and returned the ball to the 25. Three plays later an Oakland field goal attempt from the 29 went awry.

With two minutes to go, an interception by Rodger Bird, the fifth off Namath, again gave Oakland possession on its own 34. But again the Raiders couldn't move, and when Mike Eischeid punted short, the Jets found themselves in scoring territory. Here Emerson Boozer, the brilliant New York rookie running back, streaked 47 yards to put the Jets to within two points of the lead with 53 seconds showing on the clock. The Jets lined up for a two-point conversion try as the 32,144 fans in the Oakland Coliseum booed. This time the boos grew louder because of a Namath success, not because of a Namath failure. Joe drilled the ball into the chest of Sauer and New York came away with a 28-28 tie, its second of the season. With two remaining games against the powerful Chargers and Patriots, a winning season still couldn't be considered a certainty. But it was the only thing the Jets could still strive for.

Although San Diego had already been beaten by Kansas City in the running for the Western Division title, the Chargers were seeking revenge for their earlier 17-16 defeat to the Jets in Shea Stadium when the two clubs lined up for their second meeting of the year before 25,712 at Balboa Stadium in San Diego. And the Chargers did plenty of avenging, scoring two touchdowns in each of the last three periods to eradicate a short-lived 9-0 New York lead and humbling the Jets 42-27. Again, an uneven performance by Namath proved costly for the Jets.

Of the 21 passes attempted by Namath, 10 were caught by New York receivers and two landed in

Charger hands. The two interceptions increased Joe's total to 27, the most in either league. "How dumb can you be?" Namath asked of no one in particular as he came off the field after one of his passes had been stolen away by San Diego. "I never should have thrown that ball." Ewbank admitted he was unhappy about Namath's reluctance to eat the ball when circumstances dictated it, but pointed out that "Joe doesn't like to give up the yardage. But he still doesn't know when not to throw the ball and he's beginning to realize it."

Namath threw his first interception in the second period. Under heavy pressure inside his 30, he threw desperately up the middle, and Archie Matsos easily picked off the ball. That was the pass Namath later admitted he had no business throwing. On the second interception, by linebacker Rick Redman, Namath said he simply didn't see Redman coming in. On the plus side, Joe read a Charger safety blitz perfectly at one point in the third quarter, changed his call at the line of scrimmage, and looped a little pass over the middle to Pete Lammons. The play went for 53 yards and a touchdown.

When the game was over, Namath was found to be leading both major leagues in completions (218), pass attempts (450) and passing yardage (3,092). "But," a New York writer pointed out in a discussion of Namath with other reporters, "he has had only one really sensational game all year. That was the first one against Houston when he threw five touchdown passes. Outside of that, he hasn't been able to put four good quarters together."

Namath picked the season-ending game against Boston to put together four good quarters for the second time. The game had significance for both teams, particularly for the visiting Patriots, who were tied for first place in the Eastern Division with Buffalo. The 24-24 tie New York had played early in the year with Boston was keeping the Patriots out of first place and they entered Shea Stadium bent on vengeance. For the Jets, the game meant a final opportunity to finish the season with a winning record, something no New York AFL team had done since 1961.

In the first Boston-New York game of the 1966 campaign, the Patriots had blown a 17-point lead in the final quarter. This time they got off first again and led 7-0 in the first quarter. Then Namath went to work. On the first pass play the fired-up Boston defense, which had throttled Joe for most of the first game, stormed in. But Namath coolly stayed in his pocket and threw to Sauer for a first down. Namath kept on throwing, finally hitting Maynard in the end zone for the tying touchdown.

The Boston defense concentrated so intently on stopping Namath that the usually strong Patriots' rushing defense went to pieces. Namath kept calling the numbers of Snell and Boozer and the New York running backs kept churning out big chunks of yardage. By the end of the afternoon, Snell had rushed for 124 yards and Boozer for 117, both figures greater than the amount the Patriots had been used to yielding per game on the ground. Overall, New York rolled to a club single-game record of 528 yards as Namath contributed 14 complete passes in 21 attempts for 287 yards and three touchdowns, two of them to Maynard. The Jets led 17-7 at the half and matched each of three Boston scoring thrusts in the second half, when Babe Parilli began firing bullet passes for the Patriots, with a touchdown of their own. New York won 38-28 and ruined Boston's chance to win the Eastern Division crown because Buffalo had beaten Denver 38-21 to reach the AFL title game against Kansas City.

Namath had handled the team well in its final game, going to the running game when it began working well, and avoiding interceptions. "He ate the ball when he had to," glowed Ewbank. "That's real progress." But Joe did not delude himself about the season. After a promising beginning, it had turned out to be a bitter disappointment.

It didn't dim Namath's gloom when it was pointed out that, after only two seasons in pro football, he was further advanced as a quarterback than anyone since Baltimore's Johnny Unitas. Praise didn't diminish the pain in Joe's knees, which had grown progressively worse as the season wore on. That Namath had kept going at all after the first weeks of the season was incredible. "We thought by keeping him out of the pre-season games he'd rebuild the strength in his knee," said Ewbank. "But after two or three weeks it was hurting again. Joe kept going on guts alone. We noticed he was actually unable to move with any facility for the last four or five games. By the time Joe is 40 years old, he'll have arthritic knees like a man of 75. That's the price he's paying to play football."

Few outside the Jets' family ever realized the extent of the pain with which Joe had played. "Nobody ever comes out to watch practice," said trainer Jeff Snedeker. "So nobody ever realized that Namath's knee hurt so badly most of the year he could barely hobble two or three days after a game. Finally, around Thanksgiving, Howard Cosell of WABC-TV came out to watch the team work out one day and noticed that Joe couldn't even walk without pain. On the air that night he predicted Namath would miss the next game entirely. Naturally, Joe played. What Cosell saw was just the same thing Joe went through every week all season."

And, as he had suspected following his rookie season of 1965, Namath felt he needed another operation if he were ever going to play football again. This time he was right.

6. The New Namath

WHILE Namath was taking his warmup throws before the Boston game which ended the 1966 season, a reporter asked him about his knee. Joe replied that he felt it might need another operation. The interviewer then asked Joe if he would risk new surgery, "Sure Joe said. "I want it, I welcome it."

Do you think it can finally repair the leg like new, Namath was then asked. "Maybe not for football," Joe answered in a voice that quavered a little. "It can't be any worse. It can't get much worse."

After his brilliant performance had carried the Jets to victory over the Patriots, the same writer asked Sonny Werblin how he stood on the question of Namath's undergoing further knee surgery. Werblin said he preferred that Joe did not have another operation, that the knee was coming along nicely, and that Namath was coming along nicely as a thinking-man's quarterback.

The Jets' owner could not have known what was to be learned about Namath's knee within twenty-four hours.

The day after the season finale, Namath visited the office of Dr. James Nicholas, the Jets' orthopedic man. The Jets have a policy that any player who has been injured during the season must get a physical checkup before going home. The usual procedure is for Dr. Nicholas to submit a written report to the Jets on each player who has been injured, along with his recommendations, if any. Dr. Nicholas examined Joe Namath's knees and his findings could not wait for any written report. The doctor got on the phone and called Weeb Ewbank immediately.

"Coach, Namath has a torn knee cartilage," the doctor said.

"You're kidding," said Ewbank.

"No, I'm not," replied Dr. Nicholas. "It'll have to come out."

Further examination disclosed that the cartilage in Namath's right knee had been shredded in the pre-season game against Houston when Houston's Don Floyd had floored him. Though everyone knew that Joe's knee was giving him trouble all during the season, no one suspected the real extent of his injury nor the real cause of his pain. Occasionally, when Joe would come off the field with the pain on his face clearly defined, Ewbank would say, "Joe, boy, I can tell something hurts you."

"Yeah, coach," Namath would say and nothing more.

When the necessity for a second operation finally had been recognized, Namath was not the least surprised, nor sorry. "I knew all along I'd need another operation," he said. "Why didn't you say something?" he was asked. "What for?" he replied. "And miss the whole season?"

Ensuing phone calls that fateful Monday, including long distance contacts with Werblin, who had flown to his winter home in Miami Beach, didn't betray the anxiety the Jets' management felt at the unexpected turn. A tentative date for Namath's second operation was set as January 28. It was also decided that two outstanding knee specialists would consult with Dr. Nicholas on the possibility of expanding the surgery.

"They will decide," Werblin explained, "whether to do other work on his knee besides removing the cartilage. As long as they have it open, it might be a good idea to look around and see if something can be done about improving the stability of the knee."

What Werblin, who had previously indicated his reluctance to have his protege operated on, now meant was that perhaps the doctors could find a way to allow Joe to run again—at least well enough so that he wouldn't continue to be a standing target. His immobility was the only serious flaw in Namath's repertoire and, with the need for a new operation now made public, Namath explained his fear that his inability to scramble out of danger in the backfield could eventually prove costly.

"I'm no better physically now than I was at Alabama," Joe said. "Fact is, I'm worse. I simply can't run. Sometimes even when I drop back to pass I feel something wrong in the knee. You haven't got time to think about it right then but you can feel it."

That Namath was able to survive the fury of onrushing linemen—thought to be amazing enough already—now seemed unbelievable in light of the torn cartilage he had carried all season. True, his pass protection had

been good all season. But there had been that one miserable afternoon in Houston when Joe had had to scramble for his football life.

"Why are we waiting until January 28?" Namath
demanded of Nicholas. "I want that operation now.
There's no sense in waiting."

So only a week after he had entered Dr. Nicholas' office for what had started as a routine post-season checkup, and less than two years after his first operation, Joe
entered Lenox Hill Hospital for the second time. Instead of the fear he had felt two years before, Namath
felt hope. The main object of the operation would be
to remove a torn lateral cartilage, a rather routine
procedure on football knees. As Werblin had suggested,
in an effort to increase the rotary stability of the bother-
some knee, the doctors would also repair a cruciate
ligament.

Knee cartilage is described as somewhat of a shock
absorber between the *femur* (thigh bone) and the *tibia*
(shinbone). Four ligaments connect the femur and the
tibia. The medial ligament is on the inside of the knee,
the lateral ligament on the outside. Two cruciate ligaments crisscross from the front to the back. When a
ligament is torn or strained, the rotary stability of the
knee is affected. Namath's chief problem existed in the
front cruciate ligament.

Whereas the first operation had consumed one hour
and 13 minutes, the second one lasted one hour and
45 minutes. Immediately afterward, the surgery was
termed successful. A week later, shortly after New
Year's Day, 1967, Namath greeted reporters in a special
press conference arranged by the Jets.

When the reporters entered room 937 at Lenox Hill
Hospital for the press conference, they found a grinning
Joe Namath, his famous leg propped up on a pillow in

the middle of the $79-per-day room filled with flowers and get-well mementos. For his hospital tenure, Joe had grown a Fu Manchu type goatee. His hair had grown long on the sides.

"I feel great," he exclaimed. "Better than I thought I would. I'm confident about my knee. It's coming along faster than expected and it looks good, but you really don't know until you start running. There's always the risk that it might not bend far enough when I run, and then it would be difficult for me to play. I don't think what will happen four or five years from now. I just know that I had to have the operation.

"I should have more mobility and stability in the knee," Namath went on, "and I should be able to do more things with it. You don't run unless you have to; but if it's a third and eight in a passing situation and there's an opening to make the first down running, well, if the opening is there, I'd like to cut out and get it."

Joe realized that the real test was still a long way off, but saw reason to be optimistic. "I'll be able to leave here a week early," he said. "I'll be able to toss a football in February, play golf in March, and start running in April."

Joe reported only two other health problems. He discovered that he loses weight in hospitals (twenty pounds after the first operation), and his eyes had grown watery from watching seven Bowl games on television over the previous holiday weekend.

For his last few days in the hospital, Joe sat alone with his get-well gifts—bouquets, a box of matzohs sent by Toots Shor, a football game for parlor quarterbacks, and a pair of white boots monogrammed "J.W.N." The great risk he had taken in agreeing to a second operation was far from his mind, but officials of the Jets were offering silent prayers that everything had apparently come out all right. All, including Namath, suspected that even with the operation, Joe would never be able to boast of a long career in professional football. "I'm not expecting to play more than seven years," Namath confessed. "I don't see how it would be possible."

Because he felt he would have to survive on a year-to-year basis, and despite the fact that he still had one year remaining on his original contract with the Jets, Joe began thinking about asking Werblin for a $1,000,000 contract. But once out of the hospital Namath eschewed his monetary meditation and made a beeline for Miami to pursue the sun and relief from the monastic life he had uncustomarily endured for ten days in the hospital.

When Joe returned from his brief idyll in Florida, concern about his knee had abated and he resumed his social activities around New York night spots. Television and radio made demands on his time for appearances and magazine and newspaper writers sought him out at every turn. Still, Joe had time to resume his thinking about a new contract.

"I've been thinking about 1968," said Namath one afternoon over lunch with two other athletes with money on their minds, Wilt Chamberlain and Tony Conigliaro. The three of them had just come from a taping of a television panel show.

"Have you talked about the new contract yet?" asked Conigliaro, the young hero of the Boston Red Sox.

"Not yet," said Namath. "My lawyer and I have talked it over a couple of times."

"Is this the last year of your contract?" asked Chamberlain, then leading his Philadelphia 76ers teammates to the greatest season record ever compiled by a pro basketball club, but who, within two years, was to be given the most lucrative contract in the history of the sport by Los Angeles.

"Yes, 1967," Namath answered the basketball star. "I sign again for 1968."

"How does the knee feel?" asked Chamberlain.

"The one they cut feels good," grinned Joe. "But the other one bothers me, the one with bursitis."

"What would you do if you couldn't play football again?" asked another member of the crowd having lunch with the three athletes.

"I'm sure I could do something else," remarked Namath. "I've talked to some people about the movies. Sounds goofy, I know, about me and movies, I mean. But things like that happen. It sounded goofy to me when they were talking about $400,000, too. I thought that was all the money there was in the world."

Hadn't Joe expected such a fabulous offer, asked a newsman.

"It's a funny thing," said Namath. "In my senior year, just before the Auburn game, Coach Bryant came to me and said, 'Look, there are going to be a lot of pro scouts around looking at you and talking to you and you should be thinking about what you want.' I said I was thinking about $100,000 because that's what Don Trull [Baylor star signed by Houston] had signed for the year before. Coach Bryant said I should ask for $200,000; maybe I'd get it, maybe not, but maybe they'll settle for $150,000."

Namath recalled how it had been, the way the pros kept sending people around to see him after his final college game at Alabama. "The Cardinals were the first to come around," Namath remembered. "I took Coach Bryant's advice and asked for $200,000. Their scout took back the message. Then I met Sonny Werblin for the first time and told him about the Cardinals. He said he didn't want to get involved in a bidding contest, but that he was thinking more along the lines of $300,000."

Joe laughed at the impact of the memory. "Holy cow!" he exclaimed. "Just the summer before I had been working at the school for a dollar a day, keeping the baseball field in shape, pulling weeds and things."

"How high did the Cards go?" asked Chamberlain.

"They went to $389,000," said Namath. "By that time I had made up my mind I would play for the Jets. All through negotiations just one thing worried me."

"What was that?" Conigliaro wanted to know.

"I was afraid the two teams would get together and say let's stop knocking ourselves out, and toss a coin and give him $20,000."

Everybody laughed. Then Namath turned to Conigliaro. "Hey," said Namath, "I hear you went on a safari. What did you do for excitement over there?"

"I had a ball," said Conigliaro. "Ever date a female gorilla?"

"I don't think so," said Namath.

"Great!" replied Conigliaro. "They believe everything you tell them."

Joe didn't get to go on any safaris of his own that offseason, but another off-the-field development just across town from the Jets' Shea Stadium home received the same attention from the press that a Namath safari might have attracted. In an obvious attempt to combat the color and glamour of Namath, the New York Giants of the National Football League traded away several high draft choices to the Minnesota Vikings to acquire their quarterback, Fran Tarkenton.

Suddenly Namath was caught in the middle of a battle not of his own making. Who would now assume the mantle of leadership among New York's pro quarter-backs—strong-armed Joe, or the scrambling Tarkenton, who didn't have the arm of a Namath, but had built a reputation as a field leader who could pull his team out of trouble by running with the ball when the situation called for it?

Joe bristled noticeably when he and Tarkenton were compared, and they were being compared often during the 1967 Hot Stove League season. To one writer who called Tarkenton more flashy and exciting than Namath, Joe retorted, "How flashy and exciting is Bart Starr?" The Green Bay quarterback had just taken the Packers to victory in the first Super Bowl game.

"Sure, Tarkenton is exciting, and he'll give Giant fans something to look at, and the Giants will continue to draw their 62,000 to every game and we'll draw our 61,000," Namath said.

"But neither Tarkenton nor I will hold the fans on color. They want a winner, and in the end that's what will attract them. Nothing beats winning."

The weeks before the Jets' training camp was scheduled to open rolled by and Namath began to develop more confidence in his physical condition. The signs were encouraging. There was pain ("It will always hurt," he said) but Joe was growing accustomed to pain. What was *more* important to him was that he could move around in the backfield without showing signs of crumbling.

The Jets' veterans reported to training camp at the Peekskill (N.Y.) Military Academy in late July and Joe, like the rest, occupied his time during the day by playing touch football. The serious contact work was yet to come, but Weeb Ewbank and the rest of the New York coaching staff felt that the Jets' quarterback problem had been solved.

Ewbank was so enthused at his star quarterback's apparent recovery that someone teased him, "Do you think that New York will have two scrambling quarterbacks this year?"

"I hope not," replied Ewbank, flinching at the thought, recalling those times Joe had taken off and run with the ball against Oakland the previous season. For every inch of ground Namath had gained on one of his runs, Ewbank had lost a day of his life. "Get out! Get out!" he had screamed at Namath, meaning get out of bounds before those defensive monsters amputate your right leg at the knee.

Both Ewbank and Namath realized that medicine could do only so much, and that it had not yet reached the stage where it could make a scrambler or a runner out of Joe. But Namath was so delighted with the prospect for variety in the Jets' offense that his mobility would now allow, that he declared for all to hear: "The most improved thing about the Jets this year is going to be me."

As the Jets began preparing for the first exhibition game of 1967, in early August against the Boston Patriots, Ewbank started adding more rollouts and play-action passes into the Jets' playbook to make use of Joe's mobility. The Jets didn't have many opportunities to use the new plays.

A week before the exhibition game against Boston, the "new Namath," as the writers were calling him, ran back to throw when suddenly pain exploded through his left knee, the "good" one. "It felt like it wasn't going to stop for months," he said later. He tried to lean on the knee and he thought it would give way under him; he felt no life in it.

The doctors assured Joe there was nothing to worry about. The bad (right) knee was better than had been expected, and this new problem in the left knee was just the same old tendonitis, caused by favoring the right knee. "It's only temporary," the doctors told Namath, "like a tennis elbow or a tooth cavity—painful but not serious. Over the short term cortisone will reduce the inflammation; over the long term the tendon will heal itself."

Joe remained skeptical. He had suffered enough pain in his knees to decide for himself what seemed serious and what didn't. To escape the hordes of people who were either venturing opinions or asking him questions about his condition, Namath fled to New York with a teammate. They got back to camp late and Ewbank had no choice but to fine Joe $50. Some of the Jets began to grumble.

On the following Thursday evening, twenty-four hours before the first exhibition game, Joe came to see Ewbank in his office. In loud, angry voices, they argued about the fine. Joe said he wanted to go to New York; the coach refused permission.

Namath stormed out of Ewbank's office, jumped into his gold Cadillac and moments later was tooling down the highway from up state New York toward Manhattan's bright lights. Joe ended up at several night spots on the East Side, his old stomping grounds. En route, he encountered a buddy, some girls, and at the *Open End,* a club just one black away from his apartment, he encountered the sports editor of *Time* Magazine, Charles Parmiter. The magazine editor recognized Joe immediately, and, never having met him, strolled over to introduce himself to Namath.

By now it was close to three o'clock in the morning. It was not a good time for introductions. Namath, observers reported later, appeared intoxicated. Parmiter, a slight, thin man, had also been drinking. As will happen at that hour, and to people in those conditions, there were immediate misunderstandings. A witness attested that Namath grabbed Parmiter by the lapels of his coat and cursed him. "I don't like you hundred-dollar-a-week creeps writing about me," Joe allegedly said. Blows were reportedly struck. The magazine editor said they were. At any rate, within a few weeks, Parmiter was to file suit against Namath.

"I had a lot of personal problems," Namath said the next day, in explanation of his leaving camp. "I just wanted to get alone with myself. Just get alone," he snorted. "And look what happened."

The next morning, Joe, who had slept off his mistakes of the previous evening at his own apartment, was awakened by a phone call from Ewbank. The coach told Joe that rumors were circulating that he was going to quit. Were they true? No, Joe said, they weren't true. Then get up to camp, snapped Ewbank. Joe replied that he would.

In the players' rooms at the Peekskill Military Academy, the Jets sat enraged. "We felt that Joe had run out and left us holding the bag," Sam DeLuca said later. "There were rumors that Joe was holding out for more money, that he had gone to New York for some selfish reason. We didn't think he could pay a fine big enough to pay the debt he owed us. It wasn't a question of a fine anymore. It was a question of his moral obligation, as our leader, to make bed-check and to do what everyone else did."

At two o'clock that afternoon, Namath arrived back at Peekskill and went immediately to Ewbank's office. His face, unshaven, looked pale and worried. "Is Weeb in?" he asked someone. Before the man could answer, DeLuca appeared. "There's been a lot of garbage floating around," the Jets' offensive captain said to Joe. "We want to straighten out some things."

"Sure," said Namath. He went with DeLuca to a room where the players had gathered. Under questioning from his teammates, Joe first apologized for jumping camp. He had certain personal problems, he told the Jets, that he had hoped he could work out in New York. He hadn't worked them out and he had been wrong going to New York, he admitted.

"He didn't define what his personal problems were," DeLuca said later. "But he did convince us he had personal problems. We didn't condone what he did, but we believed him."

The rest of the Jets had good reason to believe Namath. What had goaded Joe into bolting camp *was* personal. He had received a tearful phone call from his mother in Beaver Falls about Bobby, his older brother. Bobby, suffering from a slipped spinal disc, had awakened to discover his legs had become suddenly paralyzed—lifeless. It was only a temporary condition, doctors assured Joe's mother, but an operation might be necessary. These were all too familiar words to Joe.

Though distraught himself, Joe tried to comfort his worried mother. He had good reason to be shocked by his brother's condition. "About ten years ago," he told a writer, "my uncle got up from a chair and fell down. Collapsed. He lay there and I remember he was laughing and saying, 'This is silly, I'm all right.' But he couldn't stand up. They took him to the doctors. His spine had just given way. I never did find out what caused it. He kept saying he was going to be all right, but I remember I went to see him in the hospital—I guess I was about fourteen—and it was horrible, the way he looked. In three days he was dead."

So Joe had escaped to New York where he felt his

thoughts could be diverted from his brother Bobby, from his dead uncle, from his own aching knees. The escape didn't help. But the meeting that DeLuca had called upon Joe's return to Peekskill had helped the Jets. "It helped Joe to understand just how important he is to the team," said DeLuca. "He was amazed, really amazed, to learn that what he did could affect us so greatly."

That afternoon, after the meeting, the Jets drove to Bridgeport, Connecticut, for the exhibition game against the Patriots. Against Boston, Joe completed four of six passes in the first quarter—another throw was dropped—for 48 yards and the Jets jumped to a 28-0 lead. In the stands someone said, "Joe should jump camp before every game."

The Jets completed the rout and after the game Joe motored back to New York City with Mike Bite, his trim, personable lawyer and agent who had come up from Birmingham, and a magazine writer, who was at the wheel. A few miles outside New York Namath suddenly let out a whoop. He'd spotted the red Thunderbird of Ray Abruzzese, his old pal, who had started out fifteen minutes earlier from Bridgeport.

On a street near Joe's east-side apartment, Ray caught up with the car Joe was in. "How'd you get down here so fast?"

Namath grinned. "Gee, we stopped twice to eat, Ray. We didn't make it so fast."

Up in Namath's penthouse some friends had gathered. They sat in the living room, a room of wood paneling, arrayed with a suede couch against one wall, an early American cabinet against another wall, fitted with stereo equipment and a color television. On the floor was Namath's white llama rug which was so thick that people couldn't walk normally over it; they plowed through it.

The color television was offering a taped replay of the Patriot game. At halftime an announcer interviewed a Jets' official. "Joe Namath," said the Jets' official, "has a real great attitude. He's always worked hard, but this year he has worked especially hard."

Joe's face broke out in a grin, his famous type of grin that spreads across his mouth no matter how hard he tries to suppress it. "Would you believe that?" he yelled to his friends. "Would you believe that?"

It had indeed been a sobering day for Joe Willie Namath.

Though Joe had been fined for his escape to New York—a fine estimated at roughly $500—Namath did not let his past mistakes rest with him. His brother Bobby was gaining strength after his operation. Joe was becoming aware that his actions could have a negative effect on the rest of the team. This awareness indicated that Namath was becoming more mature. And this maturity carried over into Joe's attitude toward the game on the field. During passing drills in training camp, where the Jets practiced between exhibition games, the defensive linemen were usually asked to restrain their charge at Namath's pass blockers. It was considered too dangerous to allow the defensive players to aim their thrusts at the blockers' knees.

But Namath felt the team was hurting itself by holding back. Joe told Sam DeLuca that it was impossible for the quarterback to get a true picture of the various defenses on pass plays when the defense didn't perform as if under game conditions. "I don't think you can give 100 percent in a game if you don't give 100 percent in practice," Namath said. After that, the drills were run at full tilt.

Joe's increased maturity, the full-scale drills, the hypoed New York offense installed by Ewbank which would make more use of running backs Matt Snell and Emerson Boozer—all appeared to be producing a more dangerous Jets' team, and a more dangerous Namath. Joe showed just how dangerous he could be in the very first game of the regular season, on the road against the Buffalo Bills.

Namath threw touchdown strikes of 19 and 56 yards to Don Maynard and New York led Buffalo's defending Eastern Division titlists 17-0 in the fourth quarter. Then, incredibly, Buffalo came back and scored 20 points in the final minutes for a 20-17 victory. New York lost more than the ball game. Matt Snell, whose blocking was almost as strong as his running, went out with a knee injury.

The game could have had a demoralizing effect on Namath. Instead Joe retaliated with a vengeance in Denver the following Sunday, but not before the underdog Broncos had bolted to a 24-7 second-quarter lead before 35,565 delirious fans in Bear Stadium. But Joe, operating behind a flawless blocking line, pitched the Jets to two touchdowns, one on a 31-yard pass to George Sauer just before half-time, and Denver's lead was shaved to 24-21.

In the second half, the New York defense caught up with its offense, holding the Broncos scoreless while Namath decimated the Denver secondary. After Jim Turner's field goal tied the game at 24-24 in the third quarter, Joe threw a two-yard swing pass to Mark Smolinski, substituting for the injured Snell in the Jet backfield, to send the Jets into the lead early in the final period. A three-yard sweep by Boozer gave New York its final score of the afternoon, a touchdown set up by a 53-yard bomb to Maynard. The statistics sheet showed that Namath had recorded his finest afternoon as a pro, completing 22 of 37 passes for 399 yards. More significantly, Joe hadn't blown his cool after the Broncos had taken the big early lead. Namath was developing, there was no question about that. Even his teammates were certain.

"Joe is getting to be a pretty good actor," George Sauer said. "Sometimes the defense will come out in a 5-1 alignment instead of the 4-3 he expected. But Joe checks off and changes the play so casually you almost miss it."

There were other evidences of football maturity in the Jets' quarterback. "We were running out the clock in the Denver game," offensive guard Dave Herman recalled, "and Joe was calling nothing but running plays. All of us were pretty tired. Any kind of straight-ahead play into the line would have used up time. But Joe came into the huddle and called for a 38-sweep. That's a wide one—lots of running—and nobody had much enthusiasm for it. Joe's the boss, so we ran the sweep and it worked well. After the game Joe made it a special point to come up to me and explain why he called it.

"Remember now, he's the quarterback," Herman continued. "He doesn't have to apologize for anything he wants to try out there. But he knew we were tired, so he told me afterward: 'They were gonna blitz inside. I could see it coming, so I figured we ought to go outside instead.' The fact that he explained it shows something about Joe. He has a good attitude, a winning attitude."

There was a new Joe Namath off the field too. "Joe has matured a lot in the past year," a friend of his said. "He doesn't go for the teeny-bopper discotheque scene so much anymore. He's better able to tell who his friends are and separate them from the ones who just want something from him."

"I guess it's true that I'm maturing," Namath said. "If learning is maturity, then I'm maturing, because I know I'm learning things. Mainly I'm learning to be careful what I say regardless what my feelings are. A lot of things I say look distorted and sound bad when they're printed in the newspapers. So I think I really haven't changed so much as I've learned about people and I've learned to be careful who I talk to.

"I still like music and I like to dance. I go out but not often. When I do go out, people make it sound like something. I can just be sitting around someplace, and people try to make something of it."

By the time Namath and the rest of the Jets returned to Shea Stadium for their home opener against the Miami Dolphins, 61,240 fans who paid their way into the ball park, setting a league record for a crowd at opening day, were ready to "make something" out of every move Joe made. The time was now, many sensed, for the $427,000 rookie to cash in.

As devastating as Joe had been the previous week against Denver, he was even more brilliant against the Dolphins. In the second quarter alone, he passed for 216 yards and he had 274 yards by halftime. If he had passed more often in the second half, he probably could have demolished the league record of 464 yards in a single game, held by George Blanda. With 96 seconds left, after the Jets gained the ball via their third interception of the game, Jim Turner, who normally did nothing but placekick, replaced Namath at quarterback. Joe had no complaints. He had completed 23 of 39 passes for the whopping total of 415 yards, another personal high. Three of his passes had gone for touchdowns—and all three were to running backs, to Boozer for 49 and five yards, and to Smolinski for 13.

Only one of Namath's passes fell into enemy hands, and that misplay occurred in the last period when he thought Maynard would cut one way and Maynard cut another. Three times receivers dropped passes in the open. "Namath called the game with intelligence and finesse," one writer noted in his story on the game. Joe had set the pattern for the game on the very first sequence of plays when he "checked off" at the line of scrimmage and threw a soft pass to Boozer for a 19-yard pickup. "I saw right away their weak-side safety and cornerback were doubling up on Maynard. That told me Boozer would be open. So I changed the play I had called in the huddle."

Again Sauer, who was on the receiving end of ten of Namath's passes against Miami, marveled at the skill with which Joe had mastered the checkoff at the line of scrimmage. "I like it when he gets that sound of urgency in his voice," Sauer grinned. "That's to make the linebackers think he's in a panic. What's he doing? Faking the checkoff and going ahead with the same play he called in the huddle."

So the Jets were off to another fast start despite the absence of the injured Snell and without DeLuca, who had been felled in a late exhibition game against Houston and had required knee surgery. The veteran guard was never to return to the active roster again.

The Jets' fast start also was helping in the race for customers with the Tarkenton-led Giants. Tarkenton was performing his acrobatics in the Giant backfield and the fans were turning out at Yankee Stadium to watch him and the rest of the Giants. But the Giants weren't winning any more than they had without Tarkenton, and the Jets hoped they could continue their winning

ways and lure the customers with their own un-acro-
batic quarterback.

Most observers felt that the Jets' next opponent,
the Oakland Raiders, would upset the Jets' winning
habit. There were still bitter memories in the New York
camp about the 24-21 defeat to Oakland in 1966 which
had followed a loss to Houston and sent the Jets
toppling on rapid slide downhill. But harsh thoughts
toward them weren't going to beat the Raiders, who
had the league's best defensive secondary and one of
the league's top front fours as well as an excellent line-
backing corps. "If there's one thing we think we can
do," said Al Davis, a one-time Oakland coach and
AFL commissioner turned part-owner of the Raiders,
"it's play defense."

This meant that the huge Raider defensive linemen
would try to beat a path to Namath, a ploy which had
worked successfully the previous season. Against the
weaker Dolphins, the New York blocking had been
so good that Namath actually had been able to pump
the ball several times before throwing. Against Oakland, the Jets' offensive line knew it faced a more
difficult task in trying to prevent the enemy from getting to its destination—Namath's body.

The task seemed even more difficult when the
Saturday evening of the Oakland game came up cool
and gusty. The wind at Shea Stadium is deceptive. It
blows in from the outfield, raises dust storms in the
infield, and does strange things with thrown footballs.
Passing against the formidable Oakland defense under
ordinary circumstances was difficult. Under the windy
conditions at Shea that night, trying to build a sustained
passing attack was impossible.

Namath had some consolation in knowing that Daryle
Lamonica, his quarterbacking counterpart with Oak-

land, would have equal trouble throwing the football in gusty Shea. But Joe knew that he would have to call on his running game to shoulder the load. Against the Raiders, who were coming off a victory over the Kansas City Chiefs, the defending AFL champions, Joe fell back on the repeated use of a play the Jets call 25 Lag.

Four things can happen off the 25 Lag: it can turn into a reverse, a pass, or a reverse pass. But usually it turns into a draw play. This Saturday night, Namath combined with his 207-pound second-year running back, Emerson Boozer, to turn 25 Lag into a very successful draw play. Boozer was to score on two seven-yard touchdown runs.

The Oakland blitz quickly took away one of the Jets' favorite plays, called 76, in which both set backs flare. But a frantic Shea Stadium crowd of 63,706, growing more certain with each Jet gain that this was going to be a Jets' year, went berserk when Namath hit Maynard for 30 yards to get close enough for the first of Boozer's touchdowns. In the second quarter, with Bill Mathis and Mark Smolinski complementing Boozer expertly in the running department, the Jets scored after one of their four interceptions against Lamonica. Mathis crashed over from the one. A field goal by Jim Turner after another interception put the Jets ahead 17-0 at halftime.

Oakland's offensive line, meanwhile, was being mauled by the New York defense. The Jets yielded nothing in the middle. Lamonica turned in desperation to the deep pass, but the Jets' pass rush was forcing him to throw hurriedly, and the wind further ruined his timing.

New York led 20-0 in the third period before the Raiders finally got on the scoreboard. But early in the fourth Namath threw the pass off 25 Lag and Mathis caught it for a 38-yard gain. Moments later, Boozer scored his second touchdown. A final score by Oakland meant nothing. The Jets won 27-14.

The Raiders claimed not to be impressed. "We were flat," said their coach, Johnny Rauch. "But Namath does have a quick delivery and striking variety—the bomb, the medium shot, the short pass. I guess I'd have to rate him the best quarterback in the league."

Oakland's fearsome 6′ 8″, 275-pound end Ben Davidson, of whom Namath had been quoted as saying, "He's one of the dirtiest football players I ever saw," didn't comment on Namath's charge. "Once I did tell him he threw a nice pass," said the large Davidson. "He called a good game."

Namath sat in front of his locker, chewing tobacco and drinking orange soda. "I really got belted a few times tonight," he said. "But the knee held up. That's the important thing. This was a big one for us.

"I was more ready for Oakland than I ever was before," Namath disclosed. "My football knowledge has improved. It's a matter of reacting to situations on the field, coping with defenses. I have a better knowledge of my receivers and better timing with them. George Sauer, for example, and Don Maynard are very different. Maynard just gets to a point, and you have to know where he's going to be. Sauer is strictly a pattern man with precise timing, taking exactly the right number of steps. You learn those things with experience."

"This was our best game," gloated Ewbank. "Everybody played so well that we don't know who to give the game ball to." Namath was as logical a candidate as any, although anyone reading the final statistical rundown on the game might have failed to realize how good a game Joe had called. He tried 28 passes, and completed nine, by far his poorest showing of the season, for 166 yards. But in calling 37 running plays against Oakland, Namath demonstrated his ability to quarterback a winning, if not necessarily esthetic, game. There was every reason to believe the Jets were on their way.

Against Houston the following Sunday, another 62,725 of the faithful turned out at Shea Stadium for a game that, despite being only the fifth of the season, figured to have deep significance in the Eastern Division race. The defending Buffalo Bills had started off badly, as had Boston and Miami, and it looked like the race would be between the Jets and Oilers.

"What race?" eastern AFL observers might have sneered during the early minutes of the New York-Houston game. The first time the Jets got the ball, Namath moved the team into scoring position with completions of 18 and 20 yards to Maynard, and Boozer scored from the five moments later. There were still ten minutes and eight seconds left in the first quarter.

In the second quarter, New York's strong side safety Jim Hudson made a one-handed interception at the Houston 30, from where Namath immediately sent Maynard racing downfield for his touchdown pass. Maynard caught the ball with no one near him. Jim Turner kicked a short field goal later in the second period to send the Jets ahead, 17-0. But here Namath and the Jets fell completely to pieces.

The first lapse created no commotion, but as things developed, it turned out to be an exasperating blunder. Another field goal try by Turner was blocked just a minute before the half ended, and Houston's Pat Holmes picked up the bouncing ball and lumbered with it 71 yards for a touchdown.

In the third quarter, tragedy struck quickly in the guise of Namath's old nemesis—the interception. On the second play, Miller Farr stepped in front of Sauer and returned the ball 51 yards for the Oilers' second touchdown. On the next series of plays for New York, Farr intercepted a sideline pass intended for Maynard and took it back 67 yards to the New York 20. Five plays later Houston scored and the Oilers led 21-17. An old but familiar sound began to be heard throughout the Shea Stadium caverns. The sound was low and hooting. It sounded like "Boo-oo-oo."

With three minutes and thirty-one seconds still left in the third period, Turner got the Jets three points closer with a field goal, but a minute and a half later the Oiler defense struck again. This time Ken Houston, beaten badly on Maynard's second-period touchdown, darted in front of Pete Lammons, juggled the ball before latching on to it, and proceeded the remaining 43 yards for the Oilers' third touchdown of the period.

With the Jets now trailing 28-20 late in the game, Namath had to continue to throw the football if the Jets were going to score. And by throwing, Namath was digging his own grave. Jim Norton intercepted Joe for the fourth time in the game early in the fourth period and, with just under seven minutes left and the Jets knocking on the Oiler goal, the ubiquitous Miller Farr corraled his third interception and brought it back to the Houston nine.

At that point, the Oiler quarterback made a tactical blunder of his own, putting the ball in the air so close to his own end zone. Defensive end Verlon Biggs deflected the ball and New York linebacker Al Atkinson stole it in mid-air and returned to the Oilers' three. Boozer barged over on the first play to make the score: Houston 28, New York 26. Then, characteristically of the wild and woolly afternoon, Namath threw for two extra points to Maynard to tie the score.

When Houston couldn't move upfield on its next series, Joe got one more chance to redeem himself. Ultimately he did, but not in the way he would have selected. Namath's pass in the waning seconds was short. It was intercepted by Houston's W. K. Hicks, the sixth steal of a Namath pass in the game. Hicks, pursued madly by New York players, dashed 40 yards from his 25 to the New York 35, whereupon he lateraled the ball back to a trailing Ken Houston. Houston went only a few steps when he stopped and lateraled to Larry Carwell.

Although by this time there was no time officially remaining in the game, the rules stipulate that a play in progress at the final gun must be completed before the game is legally over. Carwell started toward the Jets' goal line which loomed just a few yards away. There was only one more New York player to get past.

The player blocking Carwell's path was Joe Namath. But Garland Boyette, a 240-pound Oiler linebacker, closed in on Namath, intent on blocking him out of the play and allowing Carwell free access to the end zone.

Carwell never got closer than the four-yard line. Namath, to brace himself for Boyette's charge, backed up until Boyette crashed into him. Then Namath grabbed Boyette and dragged him down. Carwell, no longer able to reverse his field, fell over Boyette, the man who was going to block Joe Namath out of the play. Namath, Carwell, and Boyette lay there, the three of them in the Shea Stadium turf as the screaming crowd yelled itself horse over the final, frenetic seconds. The boos descended upon the Jets' quarterback. "I deserved it," Joe said in the dressing room. "I was ridiculous."

Namath knew that the fans would not recognize as courageous in its own right the way he had gone up against Boyette on the final play, knew that they would recall only the six interceptions he had thrown. "With a big man like that coming at me," Joe said in the locker room, attempting to be flip, "my normal path would be to go to the other sideline. I haven't made a tackle since I left college."

Namath crammed a pinch of snuff into his mouth and shook his head in dismay. "Everything was going according to game plan," he said, "until the interceptions. I felt I was throwing good. Then, all of a sudden, things started happening." Namath's six interceptions set a club record and far outweighed the 295 yards he had compiled via 27 completions in 49 throws.

"You throw two or three and they pick them off," said Joe, "and you start thinking it may happen again and it does happen."

Miami and Boston provided respite for two weeks. In the rematch against the Dolphins, whom the Jets had routed in their home opener when Joe passed for 415 yards, Namath again had things all his own way. He completed an incredible 13 of 15 passes in the first half for 199 yards and two touchdowns (no interceptions). With the Jets ahead by 24-0 at the half, Ewbank sat Namath down for the remainder of the game and allowed Mike Taliaferro to take the controls for the remainder of the 33-14 victory.

Ewbank explained that "Joe has a slight charley horse in his left thigh and we didn't want to take any chances."

Against the Boston Patriots, they of the feared pass rush, the following week, Namath fell victim to his interception problem again. The Boston pass rush was harassing Joe into hurried throws. Boston's John

Charles intercepted one of Namath's hurried pegs and returned it 35 yards for a touchdown.

Late in the second quarter, the Jets trailed 20-7 and the pass rush had forced Namath into a seemingly impossible third down and 32 yards to go situation. Instead of making the usual call for a deep pass, Joe countered the Boston blitz with a daring call for a running play. Boozer got the ball and went 48 yards before he was stopped. He scored five plays later.

The daring maneuver came at a perfect time. In the second half, the Jets' blocking returned to normal and the defense limited the Patriots to one field goal. With time to aim his passes, Namath made better connections with his receivers than he had in the first half. His seven-yard scoring toss to Lammons in the final period gave New York a 30-23 victory. After seven games, the Jets' record now was marred only by the opening day loss to Buffalo and the tie with Houston.

The beginning of the end was at hand, however. The Jets traveled to Kansas City to take on the powerful Chiefs, and learned that life in the strong AFL Western Division was a lot more strenuous than in the East. For one half, the 46,642 fans who filled Kansas City's Municipal Stadium, the largest crowd ever to see a sports event in the city, watched in chilled silence as the clubs battled tensely with the Chiefs leaving the field holding a narrow 13-10 halftime margin.

Early in the third quarter, the Chiefs conspired to break the game open behind the spirited running of Mike Garrett and the powerful pass rush applied by 287-pound Buck Buchanan and 315-pound Ernie Ladd, who had been acquired by trade from Houston before the season. The beefy Kansas City duo kept breaking through the Jet line, causing Namath to rush his throws. On four occasions, the Chiefs broke through to deflect Joe's passes. Three times they intercepted Namath, including one return of 27 yards by Willie Mitchell for a touchdown to make the score 28-10 in the third quarter. Kansas City outscored the Jets in that third quarter 22-0 to clinch the 42-18 victory.

Namath, who had begun the game smartly, had sent the Chiefs retreating with bullet throws to Maynard, Sauer, and Mathis. But the Chiefs' defense received a break when Emerson Boozer, leading the league in scoring, suffered a knee injury after a pass reception. Boozer was to miss the remainder of the schedule.

The absence of Snell and Boozer all but eliminated New York's running threat, so Namath had to pass on almost every down. He wound up with 20 completions for 245 yards but he missed often, sometimes misfiring badly, as the Chiefs' defense keyed on him.

Snell was declared over his knee surgery by the following week's game against Buffalo. But the Jets' fullback needed time to regain his form, and New York couldn't expect him to be the threat he had been earlier. Mathis, a fine blocker and pass receiver who would start in Boozer's place in the backfield, had neither Boozer's instincts for the goal line nor the breakaway abilty.

With the New York running game severely crippled, Namath became an inviting target to pass rushers, who could be reasonably certain that Joe would be attempting to throw on situations where he had previously been able to call on his running backs. Buffalo's pass rushers couldn't wait to pound Namath into the Shea Stadium turf.

The Bills' linemen did their share of pounding. Namath was thrown for 15 yards by Jim Dunaway, 13 by Ron McDole, ten by Tom Sestak, and seven by Mike Stratton. Joe could complete only 13 of his 37 passes, suffered two interceptions, two blocked passes and two tipped passes. Still, he had a good day.

When the Jets were driving, Namath consistently made a big play. His 47-yard touchdown pass to George Sauer in the first quarter succeeded despite a blitz by the Buffalo linebackers and tight coverage on Sauer.

In the third quarter, the Jets moved 79 yards in 12 plays to a 14-yard field goal by Jim Turner. On the drive, Namath connected with Sauer for 19 yards, and on third down and 10, he hit Bill Mathis for 31 yards. The second and final New York touchdown in the fourth period came on a 41-yard interception return by Johnny Sample. With Namath hurling for 338 yards, the Jets scored a convincing 20-10 victory.

The following Sunday, the Jets faced the Patriots in Boston in what was to be New York's last game against an Eastern team. Boston was in the middle of a disastrous season and even though the Jets suffered heavy injury losses in the game, they managed a 29-24 victory. Snell suffered a concussion in the first period and this time was through for the season. His replacement, erstwhile benchwarmer Billy Joe, fared better than anybody had a right to expect. Because of him, Boston had to inhibit its pass rush. Namath was able to riddle the Patriot secondary for 15 completions in 23 tries for 297 yards and touchdown bombs of 45 yards to Sauer and 75 yards to Maynard.

Given a 23-3 lead going into the final period, the New York defense seemed to relax and quarterback Don Trull engineered a late flurry that took the Patriots to three late touchdowns. But the Jets held on. Unfortunately, fullback Joe came out of the contest with a set of bruised ribs, worsening an already worrisome situation. Despite the Jets' 7-2-1 record and 1½-game lead over Houston in the Eastern Division race, the road to the throne room appeared lined with pitfalls.

No matter how great its quarterback, a team that is compelled to rely almost exclusively on throwing the football without a supplementary running game is, inevitably, a loser. Without a ground attack worthy of the name, the Jets became a loser as Namath was forced into the always perilous practice of filling the air with passes. Knowing a pass is coming, a defensive lineman can charge ahead on the snap without having to hold back for an instant to watch for the possibility of a run. He can put an extra second of pressure on a quarterback who must try to locate open receivers against a defense that is geared to stop passing.

The 32,903 hardy fans who braved rain and cold to flock to Shea Stadium for the Jets' next game against Denver were prepared for a miserable afternoon. They couldn't have known how miserable the afternoon was to become. With a week off following the Boston game, the Jets had hoped to have their runners rested and their injuries healed for the Broncos, who were mired in last place in the West. But the quick-striking Denver team exploded for 26 points in the second period by using its running backs, particularly first-year sensation Floyd Little, to great advantage. Though Namath heaved passes all over the field, the Jets couldn't score at all in the first half. In the closing moments of the second period, Taliaferro replaced Joe at quarterback for the Jets and came close to directing the Jets to a score before he suffered an interception. Namath had already been intercepted twice by Denver's free safety Jack Lentz, within a three-minute span in the first period.

The Jets trailed 33-3 late in the third quarter before they could re-assemble their passing game. Namath threw three touchdown passes—to Lammons, Smolinski, and Mathis—in the last 18 minutes, but by then Denver was too far ahead.

Namath completed 24 of 60 passes for 292 yards, the 60 passes establishing a club record as New York's ground forces managed only a pitiful 40 yards. Strangely, Namath didn't complete a single pass to a wide receiver—Maynard, Sauer, or Bake Turner—for the first 37 minutes. Maynard, who had entered the game tied for the league lead in receptions, didn't catch a pass all day. He left the game in the third quarter with a muscle strain in his left thigh.

For the first time in many weeks, there was testiness in the New York dressing room following the defeat to Denver. "Nobody had anything to do with this loss," said Namath, who had been intercepted four times in all, "except me. I fouled up."

Ewbank was even more explicit. "He had guys open," said the Jets' coach. "He just didn't hit them."

Namath couldn't be blamed for the next New York defeat 21-7 to Kansas City the following week in the season's final game at Shea. A chilling defense carried the Chiefs to victory and finally knocked the Jets out of first place in the East as Houston took over the lead. The Chiefs put the big pass rush on Namath all afternoon. They got to him five times, flooring him for a total of 49 yards in losses. Fred Williamson sealed the Jets' doom when he intercepted an errant Namath toss from his left cornerback spot in the fourth quarter and returned it 77 yards for the score that raised Kansas City's lead to 21-0. The Chiefs had broken the scoreless tie that had existed at the end of the strangely-played first half by striking for two touchdowns in the third period. New York didn't score until the nine-minute mark of the last quarter at the end of an 80-yard drive during which Namath completed seven passes, five of them to Sauer. Joe had tried to cross up the stacked Kansas City defenses by calling on his runners early in the game. It was sound strategy to try to counter Kansas City's blitzing, but the ineffectual New York runners rendered the strategy pointless. Joe attempted only 25 passes in the game, completing 14. Now the Jets, owning a 7-4-2 record, faced the unenviable task of having to beat Oakland and San Diego, two of the league's strongest teams, in successive games on the road. No one was optimistic.

But no one had to fire up the Jets for a game against Oakland either. New York had prevailed after a punishing battle the first time the two clubs had met that 1967 season, and that still represented the only defeat on the Raiders' record as the clubs prepared for the 13th game of the campaign. Some were going so far as to call the game a potential war in the making, such was the bad blood between the teams.

The game might have been the bloodiest in pro football history. The Jets could have suspected what lay in store for them when they noticed a black-and-white sign draped over the concrete wall of the Oakland Coliseum. "Classy Ben," it read, "Get Sassy Joe." Ben Davidson, his handlebar mustache flapping, laughed aloud as a fan shouted, "See if he's got his satin green socks on." There was nothing funny about Davidson's performance.

If there is any one thing that sets Joe Namath apart from the crowd, that thing is his courage. In the face of the fury of Davidson and his enraged Raider teammates that afternoon in Oakland, Namath proved his courage beyond a doubt. Determined to stop Namath this time after allowing him certain liberties in the game at Shea Stadium, Oakland mounted a ferocious pass rush, crashing in on Namath and flailing away at him every time he threw the ball.

As it turned out, Namath was tackled only once with the ball. Tom Keating, Oakland's 250-pound tackle, downed Joe for a 14-yard loss in the third quarter. But the Raider defenders clobbered Namath numerous times as he was releasing the ball. The violence and viciousness of Oakland's defense was emphasized particularly when Davidson's forearm smashed into Namath's face deep in the right corner. It was 11:43 of the fourth quarter with the Jets on their own 12, and for all practical purposes, it was no contest by then. Oakland was leading 31-14 when Davidson got to Namath, knocking him loose from his helmet and nearly from his senses. Though Joe somehow got the ball off, it missed connections with George Sauer, the intended receiver. A roughing-the-passer penalty was called, in addition to pass interference.

"When I hit him," said Davidson, "I felt they hadn't been blocking legally and it makes you mad. You get a shot at him and you got to relieve your frustrations. I guess you got to get called for it if you hit a guy in the face. But my arms were up and I brought them down just trying to block the ball."

When it was over, and Namath had made it respectable with late scoring passes to Sauer and Maynard to make the final score in Oakland's favor 38-29, Joe left the field with his right knee swollen to the size of a coconut, and his right cheekbone fractured from the force of Davidson's forearm blow in the final period. Namath tried to make light of his miseries as he fingered his swollen face in the dressing room.

"I didn't take no beating," he said, wincing as he

spoke. "I got my face swollen biting into a steak bone at breakfast." Then he grinned. "What can I say? That's what the game's all about—hitting. If you can't take it, don't play."

No one could accuse Namath of not being able to take it. Despite the battering he had received from defensive right end Davidson and the left end Ike Lassiter, Joe had one of his finest games of the season, accounting for 370 passing yards and three touchdowns with 27 completions in 46 attempts. Namath also scored once, picking up a teammate's fumble at the Oakland three and carrying it over for a second-period touchdown that gave New York a 14-10 lead.

But Oakland wrapped up the victory on two scoring passes by Daryle Lamonica within a span of three minutes and 13 seconds late in the third quarter.

"Doc," Namath told Dr. Nicholas after the game, holding his damaged cheek, "it don't feel too good."

"How the hell can it," said Dr. Nicholas, "when he got hit by a fist as big as his head."

"Hell," said Ewbank, "Joe was on his back all day and never got hit legally once."

"There are rough guys and there are dirty guys," said Winston Hill, New York's offensive left tackle who had played across the line from Davidson. "Davidson's in a class by himself."

Despite the fractured bone in his face, Namath gave no thought to sitting out the season's finale against San Diego. The Jets still had a mathematical chance of tying Houston for the Eastern Division title. New York needed a victory over the powerful Chargers, while the Oilers would have to be upset by the improving young Dolphins. It all became academic when Houston steam-rollered Miami 41-10 on the Saturday before the

Jets-Chargers clash. But Joe still insisted on playing. And he made pro football history by doing so.

Joe threw 26 times and completed 18 passes for 343 yards to lead the Jets to a 42-31 victory over the Chargers. Namath's four scoring passes, three of them to Maynard, constituted Joe's biggest point-producing day of the season. New York scored a pair of touchdowns in each of the first three periods, then stalled a closing San Diego surge to finish the season with an 8-5-1 record.

More significantly, Namath's passing total of 343 yards propelled his total air yards for the season to 4,007 yards, making Joe the first passer in history to go over the 4,000-yard mark in a season. He also finished the season leading the league in four other passing categories with 491 attempts, 258 completions, an 8.16-yard average gain per pass play—and 28 interceptions. On a percentage basis though, Namath's interception ratio per attempt was well below several other American League quarterbacks. The reason he had thrown more interceptions than anyone else was that he had thrown more passes than anyone else—64 more than runnerup John Hadl of San Diego.

Joe also trailed only Oakland's Lamonica in touchdown passes with his 26, and finished second to Kansas City's Len Dawson in completion percentage with a 52.5% mark. The feature syndicate Newspaper Enterprise Association named him the AFL's top quarterback. There wasn't as yet universal agreement on this point, but Joe Namath was coming closer to earning it —and the Jets were coming closer to their dream of a championship for New York.

7. AFL Champs

By the spring of 1968, Joe Willie Namath was a national celebrity. People who knew nothing about football recognized his name with no difficulty. But being a celebrity wasn't in and of itself a good thing to be. After three years in professional football, Namath's future was still clouded in doubt.

The offseason between his third and fourth seasons in the American League was not a good time for Joe Namath. One national magazine ran a story which held him up to ridicule. Another attempted to prove that he had gained some measure of success only because he played in the AFL, and that he couldn't have done as well in the allegedly stronger National Football League. Namath was accused of flaunting his wealth when he spent $5,000 on a double-breasted full length mink coat created by a New York furrier. And, late in the summer, Joe was accused of holding up the Jets' management for $3,000 per exhibition game— a story that began circulating after Namath refused to suit up for the opening exhibition against the Houston Oilers. This happened as an offshoot of the most drastic change among team personnel that season—the leave-taking of Sonny Werblin from the Jet scene.

The man personally responsible for the signing of Namath had been bought out of his partnership in the team's ownership after a bitter feud. Werblin rang the curtain down for himself, it was said, when he signed Joe to a new long-term, high-salary contract. The long-time agent for soap opera had created one of his own. Namath, whose relationship with Werblin and his wife, both of whom had treated him as they might have their own son, was as close as any owner-athlete relationship in sports, was upset by Sonny's departure.

Joe also was upset by the fact that his teammates, for the third straight year, had refused to consider him in the team's voting for its own Most Vauable Player. The Jets, in fact, had named him only sixth most valuable performer on the squad for 1967. This slight, intentionally or unintentionally, formed the basis of the conviction held by many Namath critics that he was not a true leader of men. Many coaches and players around the league were in agreement with this belief.

"He's too much one of the guys," many said. "He fools around too much, at practice and away from football," said others. "He's just not serious enough about football."

Despite the aspersions, Namath felt he was a leader. "Yes," he admitted to a visitor at his penthouse in the spring of 1968, "I had difficulties with some of the veterans during my first few years with the team. I had difficulties last year. But I feel I do my job as a quarterback. And if being a leader is part of the job of being a quarterback, I feel I do my job as well as the next guy."

Joe acknowledged that leadership was not something he had acquired overnight or instantaneously. "It's got to take some years of playing," he said. "If you're a rookie quarterback, you just don't walk up to a veteran with 10 or 12 years of experience and tell him what he's doing wrong. The whole thing is very difficult. Even now after I've been in the league for three years, it can be difficult. Sure, you can tell veterans what they're doing wrong and they have to listen to you, but sometimes they don't like it."

"Will it be easier for you in 1968?" the visitor asked Joe.

"It gets easier all the time," Namath replied. "The more you're with a person the closer you get to him. I'm closer with the other veterans now than I was a few years ago. It's easier to tell someone what's he's doing right and what he's doing wrong when you're close to him."

Joe then ticked off the quarterbacks he recognized as leaders. "There are three quarterbacks I admire a lot," he said. "I've admired Johnny Unitas for a long time. He's a winner. And Bart Starr, he's also a winner. And Sonny Jurgensen. He didn't have everything in the world to work with at Washington. What I'm getting at is this: You put Bart Starr at Baltimore and he'll win. You put Jurgy at Green Bay and he'll win. But what'll happen when you put Starr or Unitas at Washington?" Joe shrugged. A quarterback, he was saying, must have skilled personnel around him.

While Joe still had a distance to cover before he could gain acceptance from the world of adults, there was no

question of his hero status among youngsters. This
became obvious from the first day the Jets opened their
1968 training camp at Hofstra University in Hempstead,
N. Y., about thirty miles from the center of New York
City. Hordes of youngsters of both sexes streamed out
to the Hofstra campus daily. They poured in by bus
and by railroad and by car. Joe Namath was the man
they came to see. Autographs became as much a part
of Joe's daily training camp routine as limbering up his
arm. "He's unbelievable," gasped one high school coach,
watching hundreds of boys pressing to get closer to
Namath. "He's like the Pied Piper."

Adults weren't entirely unimpressed by the Namath
mystique either. "Hey, Joe!" shouted one pudgy house-
wife in a flowery blouse and slacks. She pulled out a
small box camera. "Say cheese, Joe. Please." Another
woman shoved a wad of Kleenex (unused) at him.
"Sign this for my kids, Joe. It's all I have in my purse."

Still, the critics continued to strike at Namath. With
Werblin's departure, and because the successors to the
Jets' president were not as knowledgeable about football as he had been, leadership of the team fell to Weeb
Ewbank. And Ewbank had not been entirely happy
with Namath over the years. One writer went so far as
to suggest that Ewbank made immediate plans to trade
Joe, saying "it is unlikely that the Jets can ever win with
Namath and Ewbank out of harmony. The athlete's
scant respect for the coach has so diminished that Namath calls the shots as to when he will play or not
play."

The detractors didn't limit their criticism of Namath
to his football. Joe's long hair, it was felt, conveyed a
damaging image for pro football. Namath's night life
came under attack again. Joe had candid replies for
the attacks on his appearance and his off-the-field

choice of activities. "You know what the real image of football is, it's brutality," he said. "Why don't they tell the kids like it is? Tell the kids that this guy is trying to hurt that guy and knock him out of the game. My hair has nothing tó do with my football. I happen to think long hair looks better, especially when a man's dressed. I used to have short hair, crew cuts, and when I had my A Club initiation, my varsity letter at Alabama, my hair was shaved off. I began to let it grow after that. I think a majority of females like a man with long hair, at least the ones I know.

"As for my night life," Namath continued, "I consider myself the leader of the Jets—the leader on the field. On the field is where it counts. Off the field it's my own life."

One incident in particular divided the pro-Namath and con-Namath camps. That was the mid-August exhibition game at the Houston Astrodome against the Oilers when Namath refused to suit up because, he claimed, his left knee was sore. A television announcer, however, reported that Joe was not playing because he had been promised by Werblin that he would be paid $3,000 per exhibition game over and above his normal salary. The new owners, Phil Iselin and Townsend Martin, it was reported, said that they wouldn't honor such an agreement.

Joe's decision not to dress for the game baffled his teammates since he had taken part in an afternoon workout at the Astrodome the day of the game, which was played under the lights. One disgruntled player complained to a sportswriter, "How're you gonna do well when you practice all week long thinking you're gonna have one quarterback, and he doesn't even dress to play?"

There was a report that Joe had told acquaintances

the day before the Houston game that he wasn't planning to play, yet had not informed Ewbank of his decision until just before gametime. The Astrodome crowd of better than 40,000 persons who turned out for the contest, which was a charity promotion, wailed loud and long when it was announced just before the kickoff that a tender left knee would keep Namath out of action. Officials of the Oilers were embarrassed as the capacity crowd hurled taunts at Namath, who spent most of the evening manning the sideline phone, adorned in a pair of white kangaroo shoes and a powder blue, double-breasted, pin-striped sportcoat.

The tension was thick on the New York bench all evening as the Oilers whacked the Jets 28-14. Joe was easily the most reviled man in the Astrodome that night. Only one friend of Joe's was known to be present. He was Jack Hurlbut, an assistant coach at Texas A&M, who had driven the ninety miles from the University to see his old college teammate. Hurlbut was the fellow Bear Bryant had excavated from the Alabama bench after Namath's suspension two weeks before the end of his junior season. Hurlbut had achieved lasting fame as the man who had replaced Namath and led Alabama into the 1964 Sugar Bowl. Joe and Hurlbut had a raucous time in the Jets' locker room both before and after the Houston game, to the apparent scorn of most of Joe's teammates. They felt they deserved an explantion. One player even approached Namath and asked him to address a full meeting of the squad as he had done the previous exhibition season after he had jumped camp. This time Joe bridled.

"No explanation is necessary," was Joe's tacit statement. "I was hurt, that's all there is to it. My knees still hurt and I can't get ready for the regular season if I keep playing when I should be resting."

When it was pointed out that people had expected him to play since he had taken part in a workout the same day, Namath explained, "I had pain out on the field this afternoon just bending my left knee the slightest bit. I threw, though, to keep my timing going; I don't want to get rusty. But the tendon could get worse and even tear if I keep going on it now."

Then Namath made a pledge. "Comes the season opener I'll be ready. That's a league game and I would play on a broken leg if I had to in that one. They're the ones that count."

Although Namath also was to miss the Jets' second exhibition game, against the Boston Patriots in Richmond, Virginia, he resumed his playing activities in full swing after that and appeared to be rounding into fine form as the opening game against the Chiefs in Kansas City's Municipal Stadium approached. Namath was also solidifying his position among the other Jets. When Namath adopted a Fu Manchu style mustache and permitted his hair to grow long over his neck, he found that several of his teamates followed his lead. To demonstrate their joint determination that 1968 would produce a Jets' championship, several players grew beards, mustaches, and sideburns, and vowed to allow neither razor nor scissors to touch their faces until the divisional title was won.

Football purists were enraged, especially at Namath, who combined his hirsuteness with his much-publicized mink coat. Though Namath sported the coat in the spirit of fun, fashion-conscious men all over New York were following Joe's lead. Others, however, looked askance at Joe's sartorial habits. One Memphis columnist grew so enraged over Namath's coat and long hair that he wrote, "It makes one wish that his hobble becomes a permanent wobble." The columnist had never even met Namath.

Joe was amazed at the negative feelings his appearance had generated. "I get letters from people saying they hope some guy cripples me because of my mustache," he said one day, shaking his head.

Namath overlooked the harsh words from fans in favor of cementing his relationship with the people he counted on most—his teammates. Joe's thinking paid off. The day before the opening game against Kansas City the Jets elected him offensive team captain, a position that had been vacant since the popular Sam De-Luca had been forced into retirement by an injury during the 1967 exhibition season. It appeared that, at last, Joe Willie had arrived.

It appeared even more so during the course of New York's upset victory over Kansas City the following afternoon. Joe threw two touchdown passes to Don Maynard and Jim Turner added two field goals and two extra points, but the key to the 20-19 victory was the maturity displayed by Namath in preserving the triumph by engineering a 70-yard drive that wasted the final six minutes of the game.

Before a new record Kansas City sports crowd of 48,871—including 2,833 who spent five dollars apiece to stand in a corner terrace—Namath had helped the Jets to a 17-3 halftime lead with his scoring bombs of 57 and 30 yards to Maynard. The powerful Chiefs capitalized on repeated New York blunders in the second half and when Jan Stenerud kicked his fourth field goal of the game with six minutes remaining in the final quarter to draw within one point of the lead, the skeptics poised for the inevitable Jet collapse.

On the kickoff following Stenerud's fourth three-

pointer, Earl Christy contributed his share to the list
of New York goofs by unwisely fielding the ball when
it appeared it was heading out of bounds. Christy
ineptly ran the ball out of bounds on the New York
five-yard line. This was to prove the final New York
blunder. The rest of the game belonged to Namath.

The clutch play came on third-and-11 from the
four after two plays had pushed the Jets even closer
to their own goal. Kansas City needed only to hold for
one more play and then could get the ball back in good
field position with plenty of time left.

On second down Joe had sought to reach Maynard
slanting across, but the ball was dropped in a loud
collision with the middle linebacker. On third down
Namath came right back with exactly the same play
and Maynard held it for a 16-yard gain to the 20.
It was a maneuver reminiscent of the days of Norm Van
Brocklin, another former great quarterback who often
would repeat plays that had failed. Later Namath
explained why he came back with the pass to Maynard.

"It's a good play," said Joe, "and Maynard was
open again. The first time I threw the ball behind him.
This wasn't my most accurate game. But I was keying
on the safeties and they left Maynard for the middle
guard to handle. No middle guard can handle Maynard."

None of the other Chiefs could handle Namath in
the last five minutes. As Kansas City's offensive team
watched helplessly from the sideline, awaiting in vain
another turn to get into the game and try for the winning points, Namath marched the Jets down the field
for 56 more yards, surviving three more third-down
situations. The entire drive consumed 15 plays, of which
Joe said, "They were almost all audibles. I was handi-
capped on some calls because I couldn't afford an

interception at that stage. I had to pass safe—and that's something I never do if I can avoid it."

Still there was one ominous note to Joe's brilliant showing in his first game as new offensive leader. Rushed hard in the third quarter by Buchanan, Namath reverted back to his schoolboy days when he scrambled out and foolishly threw an off-balance pass directly into the arms of a Kansas City linebacker. But Joe said afterwards, "I'd do it again: Boozer was open." Thus did Capt. Namath complete his first day as leader of the Jets.

Another interception of a Namath pass provided the Jets with some more anxious moments in their second game against Boston, but the Jets went on to crush the Patriots 47-31 in the game played at Legion Field in Birmingham, Alabama. The Jets' lead was only 20-10 early in the third period when Namath, with a third-and-seven on New York's 17, drifted to the goal posts, then tried to toss a screen pass to Bill Mathis. The ball was snatched by Mel Witt, a 265-pound defensive end, who ambled four yards to the end zone. Suddenly, the heavily-favoured Jets led by only three points on another seemingly inexcusable interception thrown by Namath.

On the Patriot's next series, they were pinned deep in their own territory and were forced to punt. The kick was blocked and Mark Smolinksi scooped up the loose pigskin and scooted ten yards to the goal line. Moments later, Namath and Pete Lammons collaborated on a 27-yard touchdown pass and the Jets pulled comfortably ahead.

As the Jets prepared for their third game in Buffalo, Namath became involved in another debate over what constituted good quarterbacking. Much had been made about Joe's relatively low completion percentage, compared to several National League passers.

Joe's inclination for throwing interceptions arose during the debate and Namath had his own evidence to counter the claim that he was particulary susceptible to giving the ball away. Joe ticked off on his fingers all the reasons for an interception: a bad throw by the quarterback; a faulty pattern run by the receiver; a great play by a defender.

"My interception percentage was 5.7 two years in a row," Namath said, "and compared to guys in the NFL, that was no better or worse than a lot of guys." The facts bore Namath out. His 5.7% rate of interceptions in 1967 was the same as Bart Starr's—and Namath had thrown far more passes than had the Green Bay passer. In 1966, when Joe also had been intercepted on 5.7% of his passes, that figure was far below that of the 6.9% interception rate suffered by the acknowledged dean of passers, Johnny Unitas.

"Unitas is supposed to be the greatest quarterback in pro football, right?" Namath asked a friend. "Right," agreed the friend. This was a cue for Joe to pull out an old magazine article he had been saving as ammunition for just such a discussion. Joe read aloud from the article, " 'You don't get intercepted,' said Johnny Unitas, 'if you know what you're doing.' "

Joe stared at his visitor. "Unitas said that in 1958," he said. "Two years later"—Joe flipped to another page of the article—"Unitas threw 378 passes. He had 24 interceptions, a 6.3 percent. Then in 1966, he had 6.9 intercepted and he was 32 years old then, so you couldn't say he was inexperienced. Listen," he thrust his hand into the air to emphasize his point, "when it can happen like that to Unitas, it can happen to anyone."

Namath had made his point, but had failed to take his study one step further. It might have been interesting to discover how a Unitas or a Starr had avoided interceptions in the clutch, and how they had spread out their interceptions over a period of time. Indeed, there might have been a few lessons to be learned from the study of these figures—and from the mistakes Joe had made in the first two games of 1968. If so, Namath showed against the Buffalo Bills that he had not learned them.

The 38,044 fans who piled into Buffalo's War Memorial Stadium that chilly afternoon were more interested in seeing a wake than a football game. The Bills had just been riddled by the ouster of their coach Joe Collier, and spirit among football partisans in the upper New York city was at an all-time low. New coach Harvey Johnson, appointed during the week before the game against the Jets, had no reason to feel the Bills could topple the undefeated New Yorkers.

But, as so often happens when a new coaching regime begins a team surpasses its limits to welcome the new leader, the Bills overwhelmed Namath and the Jets. The New York quarterback would have broken the league record for scoring passes with his seven—except for the fact that three of the touchdown passes were to Buffalo defenders. After George Sauer's four-yard touchdown on a pass from Namath sent the Jets off to a 7-0 lead, the Bills rallied to take a 10-7 lead at the end of the opening period. The Jets appeared in command, however, when they recoved a fumble by Buffalo quarterback Dan Darragh on the Bill's 10.

Namath misfired on two passes, then aimed one into the end zone for Curly Johnson, normally used exclusively as the Jets' punter. Buffalo safety Tom Janik picked off the pass on the goal line and streaked the entire length of the field without being touched en route to a 100-yard touchdown that tied the AFL record for interception returns. The Bills now led 17-7.

New York rallied for two touchdowns before the half ended, one on a 55-yard touchdown pass from Namath to Maynard, and the Jets led 21-20 at half-time. But Namath's problems hadn't yet begun. Joe had the Jets on the move again early in the fourth period when a Buffalo field goal had sent the Bills ahead 23-21 after three quarters. Then Namath's arching toss intended for Sauer was plucked off by Butch Byrd who ran 53 yards for a touchdown. Byrd's score gave the Buffalo defenders two touchdowns on passes, matching the total of the New York receiving corps to that point.

Unperturbed, Namath drove the Jets down the field again. This time a sideline pass went awry and Booker Edgerson grabbed it and went 45 yards for another Buffalo touchdown—the third of the day for the Bills' secondary. It was now 37-21 and the aroused Buffalo fans howled.

With time running out, Namath had to keep the ball in the air to allow New York even a shred of a chance to catch up. Namath finally enabled his own receivers to outscore the Buffalo defense by flipping touchdown strikes to Matt Snell and Sauer, but time expired before the Jets could get another drive started. In all, Namath threw five interceptions including the three that had been returned for scores, and his 19-for-43 completions for 280 yards meant nothing in the hollow wake of defeat.

The Bills had surprised the Jets—and their new coach—with their zest in physically manhandling Namath and forcing him into the five interceptions, as well as one fumble. It had been a bad day for Joe and his aching knees and no one knew better how bad a day it had been than John Namath, Joe's father.

The elder Namath had driven from Beaver Falls to watch his son play football. After the game he watched his son descend the stairs that led from the field to the War Memorial Stadium dressing rooms. John Namath watched the way his son had to use the bannisters to let himself down the stairs so that he wouldn't have to bend his knees.

"Look at him," John Namath said of his son. "He can hardly get down the stairs. I want him to quit football.

"Last Christmas he called me and I told him the best gift he could give me would be to quit. I was in the dressing room before and put my hand on his knee to talk to him. He grabbed my hand and took it off his knee and said 'Don't do that, it hurts.'

"I can't stand to watch him play anymore," Joe Namath's father declared. "He shouldn't play like that."

Joe Namath refused a seat in the bus as the Jets left the Buffalo stadium. He stood in the aisle, holding on to the hat racks above the seats. When he finally sat down, he refused to talk to anyone about his knees. He never felt more physically and emotionally drained.

Ewbank, fending off the critics who insisted that Namath should have used more running plays, told the team on the way back to New York that the next day, Monday, usually an off-day, he would review the movies of the defeat and requested all players to be present. "The pictures won't be shown on Tuesday, as usual," Ewbank said. "We'll start fresh for San Diego . . ."

The powerful Chargers would provide the opposition for the Jets in their home opener at Shea Stadium the following Saturday night. In light of the unexpected loss to Buffalo, this game loomed as a very crucial one from a New York standpoint. Ewbank was well aware that all his players, including Namath, realized the significance of the game. But the Jets' coach decided to devise a new wrinkle on his own.

In the moments before the Jets trotted onto the Shea Stadium turf, Ewbank ordered Namath to use Emerson Boozer on a sweep around right end as the team's opening offensive play. "And," said Ewbank, "let's control the ball out there."

Often a coach will call his team's opening play, then leave the quarterback to call the plays on his own. In his first three seasons, Namath's boldness would occasionally deter him from following the pre-arranged game plan. Against the Chargers he displayed the discipline he had often failed to demonstrate in the past. He listened to Ewbank. Whereas the Jets had passed on 55% of their plays in the first three games, Joe called 40 running plays against San Diego, as compared to 34 passes. Namath's ball-control leadership carried the Jets to a 23-20 triumph before 68,786, the largest crowd ever to watch an AFL contest.

"After a game like that Buffalo game," Ewbank said in explanation of his pre-game command, "you don't want something to go wrong right away. We ran the ball the first ten plays, including two penalties. Joe needed a little time to get his confidence back. I didn't want him to be forcing things when he shouldn't."

Appearing cool and collected at all times, Namath forsook the dangerous short square-out patterns that had created much of the damage in Buffalo. On long passes he gunned the ball, making certain that if the ball wasn't on target to a receiver, it would be overthrown and out of reach of any would-be interceptor. The result was that Joe Willie suffered no interceptions while completing 16 of 34 passes for 220 yards.

Two big plays late in the game settled the issue in the Jets' favor. John Hadl's third scoring pass of the game had given the Chargers a 20-16 lead. With fewer than six minutes remaining, a poised Namath shunned the use of the long pass which could regain the lead for the Jets, but could just as easily be intercepted. Instead, Joe preferred to move the ball for shorter, but surer gains. Starting from the New York 25, Namath completed three of four passes to gain a first down on the Charger 40.

From there, Namath misfired three consecutive times, but on the third attempt, Steve DeLong, the Chargers' right end, was detected roughing Namath. The penalty provided the Jets with another first down on the San Diego 25 and Joe immediately connected with Mark Smolinski, playing tight end in place of the injured Pete Lammons, for another first down at the six. Boozer tried the Charger line three times and on the third try crashed over from the one. Moments later, New York cornerback Johnny Sample saved the victory by intercepting a desperation pass by Hadl at the Jets' five-yard line and returning it to midfield with 25 seconds left in the game. The record crowd had seen a fine display of balanced football, even though there was some surprise over Namath's failure to throw a single touchdown pass.

After the success against the Chargers, many observers presumed they had seen the last of the Jets' error-filled performances. The next opponent would be the Denver Broncos and, it was felt, no team had provided as good a reason for Namath to follow a game plan as the Denver Broncos. When the Broncos had played in Shea Stadium in 1967, Joe had disregarded instructions about avoiding passes up the middle. As a result, four of his throws were intercepted and Denver had upset the Jets.

But as New York prepared to meet the Broncos again,

the ingredient that had made possible the triumph over
San Diego—the Jets' running game—was coming
asunder. Boozer was aching. Matt Snell and Bill Mathis
had aching knees. These injuries contrived also to
weaken New York's blocking in the backfield, and the
results were disastrous.

Before 62,052 disgusted customers at Shea, interceptions continued to be as much a part of Namath's
image as his mink coat and llama rug. For the second
time in three games, Joe Willie threw five passes into
enemy hands. The Jets, favored by three touchdowns,
were beaten by the Broncos 21-13. Rich Jackson,
Denver's 255-pound left end, spent the better part of
the afternoon harassing Namath as Ewbank struggled
in vain to find the right combination of blockers that
would contain the fired-up Bronco defenders.

Frustration followed frustration that disappointing
afternoon. Namath accumulated 331 yards, with 20
completions in 41 attempts, and the Jets outgained the
Broncos, 460 yards to 219. But three second-half interceptions, two holding penalties, and a determined
Bronco pass-rush kept New York in check.

On the last play of the third quarter, George Sauer's
one handed catch moved the Jets to a first down on
Denver's 14. But on third-and-eight, Namath was spilled
for a five-yard loss and New York had to settle for a
Jim Turner field goal. That kick was to represent the
last scoring for either side. Trailing by eight points
throughout the final 15 minutes, the Jets could have
salvaged a tie by scoring a touchdown and two extra
points. Instead, Charlie Greer, Denver's rookie left
cornerback, twice stole Namath passes intended for
Maynard. Finally, as the final seconds ticked off, Namath and Sauer foiled the "double kandy" coverage
that Denver coach Lou Saban had devised against

Sauer and Maynard. Sauer went deep to the right and beat his single defender for a 31-yard gain to the Denver three. However, a holding penalty on the previous play had brought about a fourth-down situation.

As the clock flashed ten seconds, Namath took the snap for the game's final play. His pass for Sauer struck the cross-bar. After this final frustration, Namath strolled dejectedly to the sideline, to the accompaniment of boos. Not long after that, Joe vilified himself in the Jets' glum dressing room.

"I ain't saying nothing except I stink," the quarterback told newsmen. "I know it's your job, but I stink, and that's it, period. I've been talking for four years and I've never refused to talk, but today I ask you to respect my wishes. I only want to say one thing—that I stink."

Coach Ewbank wasn't as critical. "The interceptions weren't Joe's fault," Ewbank said. "They were really rushing in there and we couldn't stop that Jackson all day. They were rushing Joe and hooking his arm and not giving him time." Ewbank didn't explain why Denver had not been able to intercept a single pass in their four previous games before meeting New York.

And, against Denver, Joe Willie failed to throw a touchdown pass for the second straight week.

The Jets returned to the Astrodome the next Sunday to wage battle against the Oilers, who had triumphed in the first exhibition game when Namath had refused to suit up. The Oilers had gotten off to a slow start in defense of their Eastern Division crown, but from the way the Jets began the game, it appeared that Houston would gain ground on New York's division leaders in a hurry.

Namath missed the mark with his first ten passes and Ewbank entertained notions of replacing Joe with

Parilli, the 37-year-old veteran. But the Jet coach resisted the temptation to remove Namath from the game because, as he said later, "he's the one who can get you there." Fortunately for Namath and the Jets, as abysmal as they appeared on offense in the first half against Houston, the Oilers were even worse.

Even with Namath misfiring repeatedly, New York gained a 10-0 lead by halftime on the implausible combination of a safety following a blocked punt, a one-yard sneak by Namath himself, and a two-point conversion pass off a fake kick from Parilli to Mathis. Neither team scored in the third period, but two seconds into the final 15 minutes Jim Turner put the Jets ahead 13-0 with a 12-yard field goal. The Jets, who had never won in Houston since the AFL was founded in 1960, seemed on the verge of breaking the jinx.

Then Bob Davis, Houston's quarterback, was laid low by the Jets' huge end Verlon Biggs, and had to be carried off the field. This forced Oiler coach Wally Lemm to send Don Trull into the game. Trull had an improbable background. Traded off by the Oilers to Boston the evening after Houston's incredible 28-28 tie with the Jets in Shea Stadium in 1967, Trull had been released by the Patriots and had signed on again with the Oilers as a free agent. Suddenly, the two-time castoff turned hero.

Within a span of eight minutes Trull passed for two touchdowns to give Houston a 14-13 lead. But the Jets still hadn't demonstrated any offense to speak of. Almost as if in atonement for their sins in dissipating their slim, oddly-wrought lead, New York moved 80 yards down the field to score the winning touchdown at the end of a brilliant drive led by Namath. Starting at the Jets' 20 with four minutes left to play, Namath passed three straight times to Sauer for gains of 14, nine, and

13 yards. Boozer saved Joe's fourth consecutive completion with a shoestring catch and the halfback kept moving towards the Houston 27 for the Jets' third first down in four plays.

Boozer and Snell next carried two times apiece, with the latter finally scoring the go-ahead touchdown with 45 seconds left. The Jets held on for a satisfying 20-14 victory. Namath had completed only 12 of 27 passes for 145 yards, but was nine-for-12 in the second half after an appalling three-for-15 opening half. Also, Joe had thrown neither an interception, nor a touchdown. In assessing the triumph, Ewbank said, "If we had lost, I would have had to blame it on our beating ourselves again." But Namath had brightened Ewbank's outlook by mixing running plays with his passes during the second half and had appeared more certain of his moves than ever before. While there were still detractors who remained unconvinced, certain very obvious things about Joe Namath-Quarterback were becoming established.

Because of the great strength of his throwing arm, Namath could afford to set himself to pass further behind the line of scrimmage than any other quarterback, yet still be able to throw to his receivers accurately and quickly. "By setting himself back that far," observed George Wilson, coach of the Miami Dolphins, "Joe may be helping himself see *all* his receivers better. Nobody can look over a defense like Joe. I'd rate him with Johnny Unitas as the best quarterback I've ever seen." Wilson, who had coached the Detroit Lions in the NFL for eight years before coming to Miami, was well familiar with Unitas.

So too was Ewbank, who had coached the Unitas-led Baltimore Colts to two consecutive NFL titles in 1958-59. As Namath continued developing acumen as a

pro quarterback, Ewbank now found himself beseeched
to compare the two great passers who had fallen under
his coaching wing. "John had better receivers in his
early years than Joe," Ewbank would begin hesitantly,
reluctant to reveal an edge for either man. "John is
also bigger and is able to move better than Joe. Joe has
probably the greatest release I've ever seen for getting
the pass away during a blitz." Then Weeb would add
hurriedly, "But John is good at that, too."

Ewbank's diplomacy aside, Namath had become a
passer to be feared every time he touched the football.
And as facile as his quarterbacking technique was
becoming, so too was his development as a "Put On"
artist. Joe had always possessed a flair for comedy, a
gift that sometimes got him into trouble. Once after
losing to Houston 24-0, Namath was asked why the
Jets had played so poorly. Joe gave the reporter who
had asked the question his most convincing Put On
look. "Booze and broads," he said.

The next morning, newspapers across the country
carried the story that Namath had admitted that drinking and partying were destroying him and the Jets.
"I don't deny I said it," Namath said later, "but I
was only putting him on. We just lost that game. We
came ready to play, but we got beat."

But now Joe was becoming a more adept Put On
artist, and people around him began to laugh when
the Put On was applied. During practice one afternoon
Joe leveled a Put On at Ewbank. He began by throwing
a pass against a defense that had the pass sniffed out
from its inception. "No, Joe," yelled the stumpy New
York coach. "Didn't you see that linebacker right
where you threw?"

"What linebacker, Weeb?" Joe asked, his face revealing no expression except for a quivering mouth

ready to break out into a grin. "Can't you see, Weeb?" Namath waved his hands in front of Ewbank's eyes. "You're not going blind, are you?"

"Gee, Joe," began Ewbank meekly, still unsuspecting that he had been victimized by a Put On. "I thought for sure there was a linebacker there." Namath cracked up and then Weeb knew he had fallen into Joe's trap.

Sometimes it was hard to separate what seemed like a Put On from what passed for Namath quarterbacking gospel. "It's easier to score from the 40-yard line than from the five," he told a writer one day, beginning in typical Put On fashion. "No, I mean it, I'd rather start out from further back. There are more things you can do. Once you narrow the field," Joe continued, "your choice of plays is limited. It's the same with girls," he concluded.

"I wish I was born rich," Namath told a writer. "I'd know how to spend money. Boats, planes, cars, clothes, brunettes, blondes, redheads, brownheads, blondes, just so they're pretty. I love them all. What's there in life but to relax and have some fun. Man, if you don't have it, you're not living. And *I* like to live."

Life, meanwhile, was becoming increasingly intolerable for opponents of the Jets. Namath's newly-found polish and the AFL's best defense were powering the New Yorkers to what appeared to be a runaway in the Eastern Division title race. Following the victory in Houston, the Jets returned to Shea Stadium, where they deluged the Boston Patriots with a 28-point barrage in the fourth period for a 48-14 victory. Tempering the delight of the 62,351 spectators at the absurd ease with which the Jets had handled the Patriots was the fact that Namath had watched the fourth-period four-touchdown explosion from a vantage point on the New York bench. Joe had jammed the thumb on his throwing hand early in the game when he was hit and forced into one of two interceptions he suffered. After directing the Jets to a 20-0 lead after three quarters on ten of 18 completions for 179 yards, and while former Patriot Parilli engineered the last-period devastation against his former teammates, Namath sat with his thumb stuck into a towel-covered icepack.

"I hurt it in the second game," Joe admitted later, "and I hurt it again when I was intercepted today." The second game had been the Jets' first victory against Boston in 1968. The following week Namath's troubles had begun, when he was intercepted five times at Buffalo. Furthermore, that loss to the Bills, during which Joe had thrown four touchdown passes, had marked the last time Namath had scored via the airlanes. The question of the extent of Joe's thumb injury now became a serious one. Then it was disclosed that Namath had experienced a similar injury in 1967, the week before an upset defeat to Denver. "They were afraid it was broken," Joe admitted. Yet Namath had not missed a minute of action because of injury.

Several questions now arose. Was Namath's thumb in poorer condition than the Jets were admitting? Was it perhaps the reason for Joe's frequent interceptions? In light of the fact that many of the interceptions were coming on passes to Maynard, who ran the deepest patterns on the team, was Namath having difficulty throwing the long ball?

Whatever the answers, Namath and Ewbank weren't going to permit the Buffalo Bills, their next opponents, to find out what they were. When the Bills came to Shea Stadium for a rematch with the Jets the first weekend in November, they were met by the same lineup they had faced—and beaten—in Buffalo five weeks earlier. Since that triumph, the Bills had not tasted

victory again. Buffalo's defense did what it was supposed
to do in the second meeting with the Jets—it prevented
the New York offense from scoring. But Jim Turner
kicked a league record of six field goals and Johnny
Sample raced 36 yards with an interception for the
Jets' only touchdown. The Jets won 25-21. Though
Namath again failed to throw a pass for a touchdown
and completed only ten of his 28 attempts for 164
yards, Joe demonstrated his continued growth as a field
general by maneuvering the Jets into position for
Turner's magnificent toe to go to work. Namath let
his runners move the ball into field goal range and, in
the end, his cool command spelled victory. Despite the
mediocre statistics, Joe had controlled the flow of the
game and had delivered a key play near the end which
pulled out the win.

Tight end Pete Lammons, back from injuries, was
getting free much of the game but Namath waited until
the proper moment to work the ball to Lammons. With
New York trailing 21-19, in the fourth quarter, Joe
hit the tight end for a 25-yard gain from the New York
29 to the Buffalo 46. On the next pass, again to Lammons, a Buffalo linebacker was called for interference
and the penalty got the Jets to within range of Turner's
fifth field goal. Turner's final kick closed out the
victory moments later.

Namath showed no concern over his failure to throw
a touchdown pass for the fifth game in a row. "This
will be a win in the standings," he said, "no matter
how we win it." Joe expressed satisfaction with his overall performance. "In other years, I had to try to force
the pass, but now, with our defense, I can throw it
away. There were times in this game when I threw the
ball away intentionally," Namath admitted. "I can take

the field goal and let the other team make mistakes against our defense."

Going into the season's ninth game, the Jets, behind Namath's emergence as a field leader of stature, owned a wide lead in the Eastern Division, with a 6-2 record. Second place Houston, having played one more game, was 4-5. For the Jets, a golden opportunity awaited them in their upcoming clash at Shea Stadium against the Oilers—a chance to all but eliminate the last of the competition from the divisional race. Jets teams had led the division at this advanced stage before, only to collapse under the late-season pressure. But an incident of the previous season had almost assured that the Jets would not have a letdown this time.

The Oilers had clinched the 1967 divisional title on a Saturday night in Miami. The next day the Jets, eliminated from contention, beat the San Diego Chargers in an irrelevant game. In San Diego, before the game, Werblin, then still President of the Jets, had received a telegram from the Houston Oilers wishing him good luck against the Chargers. The wire's needling last sentence, "We saved second place for you," really got the team's dander up. It's long-range effect was to fire up the Jets of 1968. "Anybody hates to be downgraded and that's what they did with that wire," said New York linebacker Larry Grantham.

This time it was the Jets who downgraded the Oilers. In the cold, wet Shea Stadium slush, the Jets romped to an easy 26-7 victory. New York took charge immediately with a new offensive formation that utilized four split receivers and confused the Houston pass defenders. Sauer, the split end, and Maynard, the flanker, were split away from the line on opposite sides as usual. But Lammons, who normally played on the line at tight end, was split wide to the left, and Boozer, the halfback, was flanked to the right. The Jets had hoped to draw single safety coverage on both Sauer and Maynard, their most dangerous passing threats, and that was the way it turned out.

The first time the Jets had the ball, Namath hit Maynard for a 19-yard gain, then hit Sauer for 43 more to the Oiler five. Two plays later Mathis scored.

Mathis also scored the other New York touchdown of the game, on a one-yard plunge in the final quarter after Turner had provided the Jets with four field goals for a total of ten in two weeks. Because of the subpar field conditions, Namath connected on only seven of his 20 throws for 185 yards and again failed to throw a touchdown pass. Of course, the ease of the victory was enough to satisfy the Jets.

But some critics remained unsatisfied. They pointed out to Namath that he had now gone six games without throwing a scoring pass. They wanted to know why. Joe finally exploded. "That's a lot of baloney. It shows how ignorant people are. What the hell's the difference how you score? I don't care how many touchdown passes I've thrown. People are making a big thing out of it. If we were losing I could understand it, but we're winning," Joe said angrily to one questioner.

Namath's point was well taken. Despite the drought of touchdown passes, the Jets had won five of the six games during which Joe had failed to connect for a touchdown, the only loss having been to Denver. Namath finally broke his scoreless streak the following week in Oakland against the Raiders. Unlike the taunting telegram which had been sent the Jets by the Houston Oilers the previous season, there were telegrams and calls aplenty after this game—but all of them were directed at the National Broadcasting Company.

The cause of the commotion was the abrupt ending of the telecast of the game to the nation's viewers. The children's program "Heidi" had priority at the 7 P.M. Eastern Standard Time slot, the network explained. Ordinarily this might have gone unchallenged, but NBC's decision to cut off the football game 65 seconds before its end deprived millions of fans from watching the unbelievable finish.

When the game was pre-empted, Turner had just kicked a 26-yard field goal following a 42-yard reception of a Namath pass by Maynard. The field goal sent the Jets ahead 32-29. At that point television sets all across the nation suddenly were filled with the sights and sounds of Heidi trundling through the Swiss Alps. What they would have been shown, had the network stayed with the game to the end, might have seemed as fictitious as "Heidi." Daryle Lamonica fired a 42-yard pass to Charlie Smith on the Raiders' second play after the kickoff and Smith scored to make it Oakland 36, New York 32. With 42 seconds remaining, New York still had time to retaliate, but Earl Christy fumbled the ensuing kickoff at the 12 and Preston Ridlehuber picked up the ball at the four and leaped into the end zone. By scoring two touchdowns within a span of nine seconds, the Raiders had transformed what had seemed like a bitter defeat to an incredible 43-32 victory.

The final seconds wrecked what had been one of Namath's most brilliant professional performances. Joe completed 19 of his 37 passes for the impressive total of 381 yards against one of the best defensive secondaries in the league. In the third period Namath unloaded a 50-yard bomb to Maynard for his first touchdown pass in seven games. For Maynard, working against a rookie cornerback, George Atkinson, all afternoon, the game was one big cakewalk. The New York flanker had a sensational day, catching 10 passes for 228 yards of the 381 Namath accumulated in the air.

The end of the Jets' four-game winning streak, particularly in the manner by which it was effected, caused some Jet partisans to fear that the team might suffer a letdown in morale and thus again fail in its bid for the Eastern title. But there was no letdown as the New Yorkers closed out its two-week West Coast trip with a rude 37-15 beating of the potent Chargers, who had still been in the race for the Western Division title before the game. Namath hit 17 of 31 passes against the Chargers and ended their title dreams. "The way Namath threw today," Charger coach Sid Gillman said after the game, "he could beat anybody."

All Namath did, in directing the Jets to an insurmountable 27-7 halftime advantage, was fire touchdown strikes of 87 yards to Maynard and 19 yards to Bill Mathis and pile up 337 yards. The 87-yarder to Maynard established a club record and went on to gain recognition as the AFL's longest pass play of the season. The New York defense intercepted San Diego quarterback John Hadl four times. Namath was intercepted but once. Against Oakland the previous week, he hadn't been intercepted at all. Thus, the stage for a new Namath was being set.

On Thanksgiving Day, New York became the Eastern Division champion—without having to move a muscle. On that day Kansas City defeated the Oilers, knocking Houston out of the race. Intent on finishing with as fine a record as they could, the Jets drove relentlessly through their final three games, though no one would dispute the fact that New York was encountering competition that ranked among the league's weakest those last three weeks of the 1968 season.

First, the Jets wore down the Miami Dolphins in

Shea Stadium 35-17. Namath played only the first half and departed with the Jets ahead 14-10. Namath threw scoring passes to Maynard, for 54 yards, and to Lammons, for five. Parilli took over at quarterback for the second half and threw three more touchdown passes, two of them to Maynard, who finished with three for the day. The total of five New York TD throws equaled the team record Namath had established on his own against Houston two seasons before. The victory over the Miami entry was the Jet's ninth of the season, the most ever by a New York AFL team.

Though the Jets had wrapped up the Eastern crown, Ewbank declined to rest his stars to excess for fear they could become rusty. In the next to last game, a 27-14 victory over the Cincinnati Bengals, this strategy almost had serious consequences. Five key New York performers went out of the game with injuries. Among the wounded were the two principal Jet receivers, Maynard and Sauer, as well as running back Mathis, offensive guard Dave Herman, and defensive tackle Bob Talamini. None was to feel the effects of his injury very long.

Namath, again playing only the first half, generated a 17-7 lead with 13 completions in 23 tries for 193 yards and touchdown tosses to Sauer (ten yards) and Maynard (12 yards).

The Jets closed out an 11-3 season the following Sunday in the uncommonly blustery Orange Bowl in Miami by trouncing the Dolphins for the second time in three weeks, this time 31-7. "First half" Namath passed ten times and completed six for 120 yards. Snell and Boozer scored on running plays. Among the injured, Maynard sat out the entire game, as did Talamini, and Herman got in for just one play. Sauer and Mathis saw regular service.

While the Jets all but sailed through their final three games after clinching the Eastern crown, the Western race was developing into a showdown between Oakland and Kansas City. After the final games of the regular season found both tied for the title, they met in a playoff the next week and Oakland's high-powered offense crushed the Kansas City defense which had yielded the fewest points in the league 41-6. Though they wouldn't admit it openly, most of the Jet players, Namath included, had hoped for an Oakland victory. New York needed no rallying cry to prepare for a game against Oakland, the Jets' bitterest rival.

But there were observers who felt that the Jets would not be as well prepared for the AFL title game as the Raiders. The Oakland team, it was reasoned, had remained at fever pitch by virtue of having to struggle through a playoff game to reach the championship final. New York, on the other hand, had not been seriously tested in weeks and had wrapped up its divisional title in almost leisurely fashion.

In the lull between the Jets' division title clinching and the AFL title game on December 29 in Shea Stadium, several significant events took place around the Jets' hangar. Two of these events were particularly significant to Joe Namath. First, his teammates elected him the Jets' Most Valuable Player, the honor he had coveted. This meant more to him than winning the league's MVP award, a trophy he was soon to realize, too. Secondly, Joe capitalized on the costliest shave in history. All the members of the Jets who had pledged at the beginning of the season not to shave their beards or have their hair cut until the team had won the Eastern title had been faithful to the pledge. After the title had been won on Thanksgiving Day, several men shaved off their beards and mustaches. But there were some holdouts, Namath being one of them.

AFL president Milt Woodard entered the picture by sending a directive to the Jets to force the holdouts against the razor into submission. The days of Joe Willie's Fu Manchu mustache were numbered. But only Namath could have made a financial killing out of its demise. An electric razor company commissioned him to shave off the growth over national television for a sum reported at $10,000. This came to about $16.67 for each of the estimated 600 hairs in Joe Willie's Fu Manchu.

Success on the football field had not spoiled Joe Willie's thirst for life during the Jets' championship season. In the course of the campaign, Namath, in partnership with two friends, had opened up a Lexington Avenue guys and gals place called *Bachelors Three.* Besides being one of the owners, Joe was one of its best customers. Along the way, Joe enticed several obliging teammates to join him in his drinking sessions. This wasn't unusual by itself, but provided Namath with plenty of material for his famous Put Ons.

"During the season [Jim] Hudson and I were drinking a lot," Namath delighted in saying, "and he said to me, 'Hey, Joe, we gotta stop all this drinkin',' and I said, 'Yeah, we'll stop drinking. We'll just drink wine.' Hudson said no, we had to stop all the way. Well, we did. So we don't drink and we go up to Buffalo and we lose and I get five interceptions.

"I go right into the dressing room," Joe Willie related, "and I tell Hudson, 'Let's not hear any more about not drinking.' Then before the Denver game, I had the flu and I didn't drink. Five interceptions."

New York's preparation for the Oakland game also fostered a couple of apocryphal Namath stories. Joe

Willie did little, if anything to deny them. In fact, Joe Willie was credited as a source for both of them. "So we're in the sauna before the Oakland game," one story had Joe saying, "the first day we were working for the game and I'm saying, 'All right fellas, this is the big one. Gotta win. Our whole season depends on it. Thinking about not drinking myself.'" Whereupon Dave Herman is supposed to have turned on Namath, yelling, "'Don't do that. Do anything but don't you stop drinking. If you don't drink, I'll grab you and pour it down your throat.'"

Practice went well all week for the Jets, as all hands reported sound and free from injury. Namath was throwing his passes long and freely and working on his own special bit of preparation for the title game. Later he recounted it this way: "The night before the Oakland game, I got the whole family in town and there's people all over my apartment and the phone keeps ringing. I wanted to get away from everything. Too crowded and too much noise. So I grabbed a bottle of Johnnie Walker Red and went to the Summit Hotel and stayed in bed all night. It loosens you up good for the game."

Namath was a poor advertisement for the loosening-up activities he prescribed. The way he began the championship game—completing only three of his first 12 passes—could best be described as anything but loose. The first quarter lasted 45 minutes, what with all the incomplete passes that killed the clock (Oakland's Daryle Lamonica hit three of his first 15), and it appeared for a while that neither side would ever get around to earning champagne for its dressing room.

Joe couldn't be blamed for trying to exploit the major Oakland weakness which had been exposed in the first clash between the two teams, the one that had been intercepted by "Heidi." That weakness was George Atkinson, the rookie left cornerback who had been virtually eaten alive by Maynard in the first meeting. Namath's first three passes in the title game were all to Maynard, thoroughly healed from his injury. Two were complete and the third resulted in an interference penalty against Atkinson. Maynard scored the first points of the game on a 14-yard reception when his sharp break toward the sideline flag left Atkinson stumbling. A few minutes later, Jim Turner kicked a 33-yard field goal to give the Jets a 10-0 lead in the first quarter, the widest margin either team enjoyed all day.

Lamonica, less accustomed than Namath to the swirling Shea Stadium winds, had difficulty making connections with his receivers until just before the end of the first quarter. Then he started the Raiders moving on short passes to his running backs and longer ones to flanker Fred Biletnikoff, who was threatening to run New York cornerback Johnny Sample off the field. Only 48 seconds into the second period, Biletnikoff grabbed a pass, ducked away from Sample's tackle and loped 29 yards for a touchdown. Before the end of the first half, the Jets and Raiders traded field goals to send the Jets off with a 13-10 advantage.

With the wind blowing in tricky gusts and puddles of mud and water at the edges of the field making the footing uncertain, the Jets were far from being safe. Especially since the ferocious Oakland defenders were getting to Namath with increasing vigor. It had begun in the first quarter shortly after the touchdown pass to Maynard had produced the game's first score. An Oakland player dislocated Namath's finger.

"I don't know how it happened," Joe Willie said. "It hurt like hell and Ike Lassiter was jumping up and down and yelling, 'Ha, ha, ha, look at your finger.' I was afraid to look. I never saw a finger like that on me before. It was bent in three ways."

On the sidelines, New York's team doctor Nicholas yanked the finger into shape and taped the wounded digit to Namath's index finger. There was no remedy for the jammed thumb Joe suffered early in the second quarter. "It ached," Namath said, "but I had to throw with it." A shot could have numbed all feeling and tampered with Joe's accuracy.

On the next series Lassiter and his partner in crime, Ben Davidson, hit Namath so hard he played the rest of the game with a peculiar buzzing sound in his head. The Raider defensive ends met each other on the right and left sides of Joe Willie's helmet. "There was a bad throbbing in my head from then on," Namath said. "But not bad enough."

Between halves Dr. Nicholas examined Joe on the sidelines, rubbing his temples and looking into his eyes. Namath was coherent, but he didn't know whether he could play the second half so he suggested that Parilli warm up just in case. And, as happened to Namath during most games, he received a shot in his left leg at the half.

After taking a beating from the Raider defense six weeks earlier, Namath had said that was football, and if the quarterback didn't have to put up with crashing defenses, "a sixty-year-old man could do my job." Most sixty-year-old men are in better shape than Joe Willie was in for the second half of the AFL championship game.

In the third quarter, the Jets' league-leading defense held Oakland for three downs inside the Jets' six-yard line and forced the Raiders to settle for a George Blanda field goal that tied the score at 13-13. Moments later

Namath, shrugging off his numerous aches, took the Jets on an 80-yard drive in which they were successful four times on third down plays. That drive ended with a touchdown pass of 20 yards to Lammons. The drive had consumed 14 plays, seven running, seven passing, all into the wind, but Joe Willie had put the Jets ahead 20-13.

Lamonica retaliated with a 57-yard pass to Sample's nemesis Biletnikoff, setting up another Blanda field goal and bringing the Raiders to within four points early in the fourth quarter. Joe Willie responded by aiming a sideline pass for Maynard, still being covered one-on-one by the rookie Atkinson. Here at last, the downtrodden rookie had his moment. He intercepted the ball and raced to the Jets' five, where Namath had to knock him out of bounds. It reminded many in the large crowd of 62,627 of the Houston debacle in 1967 when Joe Willie himself had to make a diving tackle of a large linebacker to save a 28-28 tie.

Pete Banaszak scored from the five in one play for Oakland, and the Raiders led for the first time 23-20. There were eight minutes left in the game. On the sidelines, Joe talked to Ewbank and other members of the New York coaching staff before going out to take the field for the next vital series of plays. "Don't worry, Weeb, I'll get it back," Joe Willie said. He was as good as his word, though the Jets' coach himself must have marveled at the suddenness with which Namath was to strike.

It was in a series of three plays that Joe showed the true coolness of a champion. Starting on the New York 32, Namath began with a down-and-out to Sauer for ten yards. Then Joe combined with Maynard on a perfect play that even the greatest of defensive backs could not have prevented. The Jet flanker sprinted down the sideline with the rookie Atkinson at his heels, and Namath's pass simply fell into Don's hands downfield for a 52-yard gain to the Oakland six. From there Joe called a play-action pass in which he had various options as he watched the play unfold after the snap. He looked for Bill Mathis swinging toward the flag, turned, and drilled a hard line drive pass to Maynard in the end zone. Within 31 seconds the Jets were again in front 27-23.

The Raiders had two more chances to win, but Coach Rauch committed a blunder on the next series that may have cost his team the victory. Oakland had the ball on the Jet 26, fourth down and ten. Normal strategy, with a kicker like George Blanda available, dictated a field goal which would have reduced New York's lead to one point with plenty of time left to get the ball back and score again.

Rauch disregarded the fact that Lamonica was moving the team very well, and likely could have done so again on another series. He directed his quarterback to try to convert the nearly impossible fourth-down situation. Lamonica never had a chance. New York right end Verlon Biggs faked to the inside, leaped around a blocker and smothered Lamonica for a loss. Instead of a reasonably certain three points, the Raiders had nothing. Now they needed a touchdown to win.

Lamonica, performing heroically under pressure conditions, nearly accomplished the miracle. With two minutes left, he found Biletnikoff and Warren Wells for two long completions, and a penalty moved the ball to the New York 24. Again Lamonica faded back. Three receivers were covered so he threw a safety-valve pass to running back Charlie Smith. The ball was behind Smith, who himself was behind Lamonica, making the pass a lateral rather than a forward pass.

Jet linebacker Ralph Baker grabbed the loose ball and the Jets survived the final two minutes. The championship was theirs. The supremely confident Namath assured newsmen and friends that New York could still have won even had the Raiders been able to score on either of their final drives. "If we had to we would have scored," Joe Willie said.

As he had done so often during the championship season, Namath had to save the day for the Jets in the locker room. AFL president Milt Woodard, in the past a staunch opponent of overly hairy Jets, tried to bar the victors from their spoils—oceans of champagne.

"Hey Milt," a Jets employee said, "the champagne is in the back room. Help yourself."

"No, no, cut it off, there's a league rule against champagne in the locker room," Woodard said feebly.

Namath was having none of this. This was the Jets' day and no one was going to stop them from their due celebration. "O.K., Weeb," he said to Ewbank as Woodard approached them, "Where'd you hide the champagne?"

"There's twenty-five cases in the back," replied Ewbank, a wide grin spreading over his pudgy face.

"That ought to be enough," Joe Willie said. "Excuse me, please. Let me through." He squeezed past Woodard. "Oh, hell," said the AFL president. The rest of the Jets followed.

Throughout all the champagne drinking there was controlled joy in the New York dressing room. There was one sobering thought in the minds of the Jet players. The Baltimore Colts were facing the Cleveland Browns the same day for the National League title and the Jets knew they still had one more game coming up

—the big one, the Super Bowl—against the winner of the NFL crown. This realization tempered the joy.

Someone asked Namath if he was planning to take any time off. "I'll be out here tomorrow," replied Joe Willie. "We've got some important work to do."

Like the other Jets, Namath refused to be lured into expressing a preference for either the Browns or Colts as Super Bowl opponents. "What's the score now?" he asked. "17-0," somebody answered.

"I guess it'll be Baltimore," he remarked to no one in particular. As he spoke, the Colts were continuing to move toward a 34-0 stampeding of the Browns. This was a Baltimore team which ranked among the greatest in NFL history, a team with a powerful offense and an almost impregnable defense that featured neither a "fearsome foursome" nor a "gruesome two-some," but an "illegal eleven." It was a team to be feared.

8. Super Joe

NAMATH did not fear the Baltimore Colts.

Where pro football people had them as supermen in cleats, Joe Willie did not. What's more, he made his feelings known in the locker room after the Jets had won the AFL championship.

Speaking about the quarterback of the Colts, Earl Morrall, he said, "Hell, we've got four quarterbacks better'n him in our own league."

"Izzat so?" asked a writer. "Who?"

"Well," Namath said, "I gotta go with John Hadl of the Chargers, Daryle Lamonica of the Raiders, Bob Griese of Miami . . . and"—nonchantly—"myself."

For pro football traditionalists, such talk was suicidal. Before the first Super Bowl between Kansas City and Green Bay, a K.C. defensive back, Fred Williamson, fondly described the crushing blows he administered to pass receivers with his forearm, a tactic he referred to as "the hammer." Williamson suggested that once the Packers got a few raps of the hammer, their pass attack would be finished for the afternoon. The way it had ended was that Williamson had to leave the game early when the Packers knocked him senseless.

Such incidents were constantly evoked by pro coaches as evidence that pregame rhetoric could incense the foe, a notion to which Namath did not adhere.

Nor did he adhere to conventional ways on a social level either. On a night twenty-four hours before New Year's Eve, he attended a celebration party in the Diamond Club of Shea Stadium given by the club. Joe was impeccably dressed in his striped gray, double-breasted six-button suit with the wide lapels—quite different from the standard cuts worn by most of his teammates. What Joe had to say at the affair was also different. While other players remarked on the loyal support of their wives, Namath quipped, "Like they say, wives must be wonderful. But, personally, in appreciation for what they did for me this year, I want to thank all the broads in New York."

What Joe had to say about the Super Bowl remained just as offbeat. On the flight to Florida, Namath held an impromptu press conference.

"Did you really mean what you said about Lamonica and Morrall and the other AFL quarterbacks?" one of the reporters asked.

"Absolutely," said Namath.

"But isn't this going to fire up the Colts?"

"Listen," said the Jets' quarterback, "if they need this kind of stuff as incentive to play us, they're in trouble already."

The Jets, meanwhile, were planning how to handle

the troubles that arise on the field. Offensive coach Clive Rush briefed the team on the Colts' defensive tendencies. The Colts' defense, rated the best in football, liked to stunt and slant (shift about) and the linebackers often bolstered a pass rush by blitzing. Its secondary favored a zone defense, in which players covered certain portions of the field rather than covering individual men. It was defense calculated to curb the long pass.

Watching the films of the Colts' games, Namath was even more convinced that Baltimore could be beaten, an appraisal not shared by the oddsmakers—they made the NFL champs 19 point favorites. Already though, Namath was figuring what he would do against Baltimore.

First, he would establish the Jets' ground game—by sending Matt Snell and Emerson Boozer at the Colt defense. The most vulnerable part of the Baltimore line appeared to be its right side where thirty-six-year-old Ordell Braase was matched against New York's Winston Hill, a big, quick tackle.

Once the Colt line was anchored by the threat of the run, Namath didn't figure there were defenders anywhere who could stop Maynard and Sauer. That meant the Colts would blitz him to stop the pass. The blitz didn't worry Joe. He could release the football quicker than any quarterback in the game.

The early practice sessions in Florida were arduous. Ewbank wanted the team at peak condition for the game —and well rested. He ordered an 11 P.M. curfew. It didn't bother Joe—he wasn't lonely in the days before the game. His father arrived from Beaver Falls. So did a blonde coed who went to school in Pensacola and was a frequent companion of Joe Willie's in Florida and

New York. Ewbank didn't mind; he figured they'd keep Namath out of trouble.

Of course, he was wrong. For on the Sunday before the game, Namath ran into several Colts at Fazio's, a restaurant on the main drag in Fort Lauderdale. Among them was Lou Michaels, the Baltimore place-kicker and brother of Jet defensive coach Walt Michaels. Walt had vowed not to speak to Lou for fear of inadvertently passing on information to him. But the ban did not apply to Namath, who commenced to needle big Lou. The dialogue—later reconstructed—went like this:

"Hello, Joe," said Michaels.

"We're going to kick hell out of the Colts," said Namath.

"Haven't you heard of the word modesty, Joseph?"

"I'm going to pick you apart."

"It's kind of hard, Joseph, throwing out of a well and finding receivers."

"Don't worry—my blockers will give me plenty of time."

"Well, if we get in trouble, we can send in the master [John Unitas]."

"I hope you have to, because that would mean the game is too far gone."

By now, Michaels was fuming, and was ready to settle the difference of opinions with his fists. Eventually, though, tempers cooled and the parting was amicable—especially when Namath paid the tab for everybody—Colts and Jets alike—by peeling off a hundred dollar bill.

But his gesture didn't appease the Colts for long. The more they thought of what Namath had said, the more they resented it. When Baltimore coach Don Shula was reminded about Namath's evaluation of

Morrall, he snapped, "How Namath can rap Earl is a thing I don't understand. How do you rap a guy who's NFL Player of the Year?"

Namath, however, didn't stop rapping. At a football banquet in Miami Springs Villas, Joe raised a drink and told the audience: "The Jets will win Sunday! I guarantee it."

There was a hiss from the rear of the room.

"Who's that?" Namath asked, smiling. "Lou Michaels?"

By now, Namath was on a super spot. He'd roused the dander of the prideful Colts to the point where there were broad hints that he would finish the game the way Kansas City's Williamson had—on his backside.

What Namath had intended by all his talking was not clear, he never did say. The thinking among some pro football people was that it was a calculated attempt to bolster the confidence of his teammates, long suffering from an AFL inferiority complex.

Another interpretation was that Namath wanted to brainwash the Colts. "You know why Joe is doing all this talking?" a friend of his said. "He not only wants the Jets to believe the way he does, that they can beat Baltimore, but also he wants to fire up the Colts. Sure, that may sound preposterous, but Joe has watched films, a lot more hours than most people realize, and he knows the Colts can't get to him. He wants to make them so mad that they'll practically commit suicide trying to reach him. That way, when they find out they can't touch him, they'll feel very frustrated and let down. He wants them to throw all their blitzes at him so he can hit the quick passes and make the Colts lose their poise. Joe is not exactly stupid."

Such a plan was remarkably similar to what heavy-weight boxer Cassius Clay had done to the champion,

Sonny Liston, before their first fight. In prefight confrontations, Clay had teased and taunted him so that Liston would want to knock his head off as quickly as he could. When Sonny had discovered he couldn't lay a glove on Clay, he lost heart . . . and the fight.

But the oddsmakers didn't figure that would happen to Baltimore. Namath's posturing had turned the game into a grudge affair—in certain quarters the Colts were made 21-point favorites. Baltimore was thought to be angry. Namath and New York were thought to be in for trouble.

None of this bothered Namath. "One thing a quarterback can't do is to get all emotional about a game before he goes out there," he said. "At Alabama, we'd ride down from Tuscaloosa to Birmingham the day before a game, and if someone would drop a pin on that bus it'd go 'boing' like a shot put. I couldn't eat I was so nervous.

"In the pros, I learned that if you've got 'I got to win,' or 'what are we going to do if we lose?' in your mind, there's no room for reading the defenses and all the other things you need to beat a good team."

So Joe Willie remained cool and confident before the game—much to the satisfaction of Ewbank, who said, "I don't think any player should start a game or even show up if he doesn't think he has an opportunity to win."

On Super Sunday, January 12, 1969, he was good and ready. The Orange Bowl was packed with 75,377 people, including astronauts Frank Borman, Jim Lovell and Bill Anders, who'd just returned from a close inspection of the moon, a spectacle that Namath and teammates shortly would rival for excitement.

In the Jets' dressing room, Ewbank was saying, "If we get scored on early, which can happen to you in a game like this, we'll go out and get two. So don't let anything that might happen upset you. If we get one first, we'll go out and get a second one to give us a cushion. But if we happen to get behind, don't go crazy."

Ewbank's warning was based on events in the previous two Super Bowls. In both games, the AFL teams (Kansas City and the Oakland Raiders) had lost by departing from their game plans upon relinquishing the lead. "I thought they lost the games because they lost their poise," Ewbank said.

New York was poised from the start. Earl Christy ran the kickoff back to the Jets' 23, from where Namath called *19 Straight,* a running play in which Snell carried the football into the right side of the Baltimore line.

Tackle Hill drove Braase, the right defensive end of the Colts, to the inside and Snell veered wide. He made three yards before Don Shinnick, the right corner linebacker, knocked him down.

On the next play—another 19 Straight—Snell's hole was inside Braase, so he lowered his head and charged through for 9 yards. Baltimore safetyman Rich Volk rushed up to make the tackle, and did—but not without regrets. Snell hit him so hard that Volk had to leave the field for awhile. (After the game, Volk's head was still ringing from the blow that Snell had delivered, and he was sent to the hospital with what was diagnosed as a brain concussion.)

The 19 Straight was a key to the Jets' attack that afternoon. "We thought we could run against them," Ewbank said afterwards, "but we had to be careful where we did it. They had Bubba Smith at left end and we had moved Dave Herman over from guard to right tackle to play opposite him. We wouldn't expect

Dave to do as well over there. And Randy Rasmussen, the guard next to him, does a good job, but he's still a young kid. So, basically, we set our offense to go at their right side. A lot of people thought we were picking on Braase. Not actually. Later on, they said he had a bad back. We didn't know it. We did know we had a real good blocker opposite him in Hill."

For strategic purposes, however, Namath tested the other side of the Baltimore line, too. It didn't work. Boozer was tackled for a four-yard loss. And with second and 14 from his 31, Namath was forced to pass. Not unexpectedly, the Colts blitzed. Namath was waiting for it. He threw a short pass to Boozer in the right flat for nine yards. It was not enough for a first down and, when a running play failed on third down, New York had to punt.

The Colts took over their own 27. It didn't take them long to move the football. On the first play, Morrall threw a look-in pass to tight end John Mackey, a receiver with a reputation for running over people once he'd caught the football. Mackey ran over people and made nineteen yards before he was stopped.

Then the Colts ran the ball three straight times— all the way to the New York 31 for a first down. From there, Morrall hit Tom Mitchell with a pass to put the ball at the 19—as far as Baltimore would get on the drive. When New York's defense resisted, Baltimore's Michaels came in to kick a field goal. His kick from the 27 missed.

Four plays later, Namath went for the touchdown. Maynard sprinted down the field on a fly pattern and accelerated past the lone defender, Colt safety Jerry Logan. The crowd rose to its feet as Joe threw a long arching pass toward the goal line. If Maynard could get to it: touchdown. Hampered by a pulled leg muscle, he just missed catching the football.

(After the game, Maynard told the quarterback, "I'm sorry about the long one, but I was hurting." And Joe said, "Man, you should have told me before the game and I could have taken a little off the ball.")

But the play had been useful to New York. For it had made the Baltimore defense conscious of the Namath-Maynard combination, so much so that thereafter the zone defense was shaded to Don's side of the field, leaving George Sauer free. It was a situation that Namath recognized right away.

"He just let me entertain my guys [cornerback Bob Boyd and occasionally Logan doubling up]," said Maynard, "and concentrated on Sauer."

The strategy did not work at first. Just before the end of the quarter, Sauer fumbled a pass thrown to him by Namath and Baltimore linebacker Ron Porter recovered on the New York 12.

It was the first break of the game, and Morrall went for the touchdown on the next play. Mitchell was open in the end zone, but Jet linebacker Al Atkinson deflected the ball so that it caromed off the Colt's shoulder pads and spiralled into the air. Randy Beverly, the trailing cornerback, dove for the ball and caught it for an automatic touchback and reprieve for the Jets. New York got the ball at the 20.

"Okay," Namath said, "19 Straight."

The Jets smacked their hands in unison and broke from the huddle. Namath crouched over center and eyed the defense. Then he called signals. The ball came back, and Joe put it out for the hard-driving Snell. The Jet fullback whirled into the vulnerable right side of the Colt line and ripped away from grasping hands for a gain. Three times it was Snell on 19 Straight, powering his way past the befuddled Baltimore defenders for a first down.

The situation was right for a pass now. Namath took the ball and skipped back a few steps, as if to throw. Predictably, the Colt linemen came driving through to get at their tormentor. They never did. For on his way back into the pocket, Namath had thrust the ball into Snell's belly on a draw play, and Matt sped through the middle for 12 yards to the New York 46.

Ewbank ordered Snell to the sidelines, where he inhaled from an oxygen device to revive his strength. In Snell's absence, Namath put the ball into the air. The Colts anticipated that, and blitzed. It didn't work. Namath dumped the ball to Bill Mathis, Snell's replacement, who ran with it across midfield.

The Colts returned to a more conventional pass rush, which gave Namath time to throw to Sauer. He did, first on a turn-in pass for 14 yards then on a square-out for 11. The Jets were on the move.

Boozer carried the ball for two yards to the 21, and again Baltimore anticipated that Namath would throw. So the Colts blitzed to reverse the momentum of the drive. But Namath reacted with the cool of a tightrope walker. He allowed the lineman to advance on him and then threw to Snell over the middle for 12 yards and a first down at the nine.

For most of the game, Namath had been avoiding tackle Fred Miller and 295-pound Bubba Smith, the strong side of the Colt line. But now he sent Snell right at them, and Matt drove all the way to the 4-yard line.

Then Namath directed the attack at the Colts' weak side. Snell took the ball again and headed off tackle. But when no hole opened, he bellied wide and raced untouched into the end zone for the touchdown. An AFL team led for the first time in the history of the Super Bowl: New York 7, Baltimore 0.

The game was far from over, but suddenly the Colts realized that this Super Bowl was going to be different from the others. "We should have had points on the board with the way we moved the ball, and we were behind 7-0," said one Colt afterwards. "We should have stuck to the game plan, but we began to panic. That's what they were supposed to do, but they didn't."

There was no doubt about it. Namath had psyched the Colts. They had taken him for a loudmouth without the resources to back his words. But the kid was playing like an astute veteran, and Baltimore began to flounder.

Big Mackey was banged so hard by the Jets' cornerback John Sample that he couldn't hang on to the football when it was thrown to him. Left-footed kicker and debater Michaels missed his second field goal of the afternoon, this time from the 46. And Morrall missed just about everybody.

From the New York 16, Earl tried to hit Willie Richardson in the end zone on a slant-in pattern. But the ball was thrown low and wide, and Richardson never had a chance for it. But Sample did, and he intercepted the ball and fell to the ground.

Then, in the last minute of the half, Morrall missed again, on a razzle-dazzle play that fooled the Jets. The ball was on the New York 41 with 25 seconds left in the half when Morrall handed off to Matte.

Matte swept to his right, as if to run. Then he stopped, pivoted toward Morrall and threw the quarterback an overhand lateral. By now, the New York defenders were scattered across the field, and Baltimore's Jimmy Orr was standing downfield alone, waving like a traffic cop.

"I was open from here to Tampa," Orr would say afterwards.

Everybody in the ballpark but Morrall saw Orr. He saw fullback Hill instead, and threw over the middle and deep to him. But here came New York defensive back Jim Hudson to snatch the football from the air and enable the Jets to go to the locker room with a 7-0 halftime lead.

For Namath, it was a superb first half of quarterbacking. Ewbank warned the quarterback to keep the pressure on the Colts. "We don't want to sit on a lead," he said. "Not in a game like this. Let's assume we're seven points behind instead of seven points up. And stick with our game plan."

Namath had a chance to apply the pressure sooner than he expected. For on the Colts' first play from scrimmage in the second half, Matte fumbled and New York's Ralph Baker recovered the ball. Namath drove the team for two first downs, and when the attack faltered, Jim Turner kicked a 32-yard field goal to make the score 10-0.

Joe Willie had thrown the Colts into a funk. Morrall indicated that when he abandoned Baltimore's more conservative tactics and threw the ball deep on first down, it was a sure sign that the Colts no longer trusted their ability to handle the New Yorkers' line.

It was also a sign of Morrall's desperation. For as he worked against the Jets' defense, there was Johnny Unitas on the sidelines warming up. Unitas had suffered an elbow injury early in the season and had been on the bench all year. The elbow had healed to a degree, enough at least so that he could play.

Meanwhile, Morrall had failed in his last try at getting the Colts a score, and New York had the football.

Again, Namath moved the team, outguessing the famed Colts' defense play after play.

"Namath was really something," Jet guard Bob Talamini said later. "We'd get in the huddle and he'd call, 'play at the line.' That meant we didn't have a set play—he'd call it when we got up to the line. I'd say he did it 40 to 50 percent of the time."

New York marched all the way to the Baltimore 23, from where Namath decided to go to Maynard for the second time that game. Again he arched a pass toward the end zone and again Maynard raced toward it. This time he caught it, but it didn't count: he'd run beyond the end line before he'd gotten his hands on the football.

What's more, on the same play Namath smacked his thumb on the shoulder pads of the onrushing Fred Miller with such force that he rushed to the sidelines and signalled for Parilli to replace him.

"I could have let it go," he said later, "but I thought it would be better to have Babe in there for a play or two while the pain left."

Parilli passed to Sauer on a third-down situation, but it was incomplete. So Turner came in to kick a field goal that made the score 13-0.

By now, Unitas was in the game, but the old magic was gone. On his first series of downs, he failed to get the Colts moving and Baltimore had to kick.

New York started to drive again. Namath's passes to Sauer gained 50 yards and, when the third quarter ended, the ball was on the Baltimore 6. Joe jogged to the sidelines to talk to Ewbank.

"What do you think, Weeb?" he asked. "Shouldn't we be sure to get the three points and not make a mistake?"

"I agree with you wholeheartedly, Joe," said Weeb. "Play your game but don't have an interception."

Namath didn't bother passing the ball. When three running plays produced only three yards, Turner proceeded to kick his third field goal of the game. New York 16, Baltimore 0.

It was all over now. Unitas got the Colts a touchdown, but that was the extent of Baltimore scoring for the day. When the final gun sounded, it was New York 16, Baltimore 7. And there was Joe Willie Namath trotting off the field, one finger raised symbolically to indicate that the Jets were number one. SuperJoe had done what he had said he would: he'd brought the New York Jets a world championship.

He had completed 17 of 28 passes for 206 yards, and called such an intelligent game that even the downtrodden Colts gave him credit afterwards.

Said Colt lineman Billy Ray Smith: "He did it all. He threw the ball short a little. He threw the ball long a little. He ran the ball a little. He had it all going and so they won."

"He was all we had heard," said Baltimore coach Shula. "A fine football player."

Indeed he was—and he was proud of it. "A guy who doesn't have confidence," Joe said, "just doesn't come from a good family."

There was only one thing that bothered Joe: the locker room prohibition against champagne was being heeded. "I want to say this," SuperJoe said, "No champagne for the world champions is ridiculous. I never saw anything like that. Of course, I was never a world champion before."

9. In His Prime

Joe Namath turned 30 on May 31, 1973.

This might have made him a new enemy of the under-30 generation, but Joe was entering the prime of his life and, many believed, his football career. If these observers were correct, then Namath would continue to rise in stature as the hottest sports celebrity in the United States.

Namath already had come close to moving mountains on the strength of his personality and charisma. In 1970, largely as a result of the Jets' 1969 Super Bowl victory engineered by Namath, the National and American Football Leagues merged into one 26-team National Football League. The Jets joined a five-team grouping called the American Conference's Eastern Division.

Even in the early stages of his career with the Jets,

Joe had been labeled a future movie possibility. And in the early 1970s he became a star in films, with leading roles in three major movies—"Norwood" with Glen Campbell, "G. C. and Company" with Ann-Margret, and "The Last Rebel" with Clint Eastwood. Namath received favorable notices for all three acting roles, particularly for his performance in "G. C. and Company," a motorcycle epic.

In addition to his breakthrough in films, Joe achieved a breakthrough in all-round finances for football players. Before the 1972 season he signed a new two-year contract with the Jets that called for him to receive an annual salary of $250,000 from the team. This reportedly was the largest wage ever earned by a pro football player.

Namath's potential for income outside of his football earnings also was vast. "If Joe accepted even half the offers that come his way every year," said a spokesman for the Jets, "there'd be no limit to the amount of money he could make. As it is, he's very selective. There are things he'll endorse because they're products kids like—a popcorn maker and a chocolate drink, for example. Then there are types of clothes he personally likes, and other types of products—typewriters, shaving cream, and so on."

In the spring of 1972, a trade paper for the advertising industry reported that Namath was the star of three commercials that ranked in the top 100 of all commercials. The paper also reported that his endorsement of a particular brand of shaving cream was one of the most lucrative commericals ever made.

Joe's appearances on nationwide television were by no means limited to commercials. For two seasons he had a syndicated talk show, in which he exhibited a gift for repartee and good-humored conversation with guests from all fields of endeavor. He also made frequent guest shots on such major TV attractions as "The Johnny Carson Show," where he appeared as a guest, and as a substitute host on "The Flip Wilson Show," "Laugh-In," "The Dinah Shore Show," and the annual Academy Awards presentations. He even made regular —unpaid—appearances on the "Sesame Street" program for pre-school children, and seemed to enjoy being around three- and four-year-olds.

Though he was forced to divest himself of his interest in the Bachelors III restaurant in New York—by order of pro football Commissioner Pete Rozelle before the 1969 regular season—Namath still retained three restaurants of the same name in Boston; Fort Lauderdale, Florida, which was his winter home; and Tuscaloosa, Alabama, near the site of his college campus. Investigation by the Commissioner's office of the three restaurants apparently turned up few or none of the allegations that had been made about Joe's New York eatery. When Rozelle had ordered Namath to give up the location in Manhattan's East Sixties and Second Avenue, he declared that "undesirable elements" were known to be habitués of the restaurant, and that Joe would risk suspension from football unless he relinquished his interests in the establishment.

During the summers, before the time came to report to training camp with the Jets, Namath operated an instructional football camp on New York's Long Island for young boys, one of the most popular football camps in the country. John Dockery, a one-time teammate of Joe's who played in the Jets' defensive backfield for four years, was the supervising instructor during the camp's daily sessions, although John was traded to the Pittsburgh Steelers early in the 1972 campaign.

Namath was the first to acknowledge the benefits

football had brought to his life. "Football has been great for me," he told a friend one fall afternoon in 1972. "It's been everything in life to me. When I was growing up, my mother was a maid in Patterson Heights, the fancy section of Beaver Falls. At midnight she'd stay up late, cutting down my brothers' old football and baseball uniforms to fit me. Now my mother lives in Patterson Heights.

"There are so many great things about football," Joe continued. "You learn discipline and dedication, and there's a lot of competitive spirit. You can't cheat anybody out there. Football is a humbling game and even humiliating sometimes. But I'd like to play as long as I can."

As he gracefully accepted the advent of his 30th birthday, a smiling Namath even admitted that marriage was in his future, a fact that couldn't have rested easily with the thousands of Namath-worshippers among New York's fairer set. "Sure, I'd like to settle down some day," Joe confessed. "I'd like to have a lady put up with me, raise a family, set up a house, have a home."

Professionally speaking, if he followed the lead of many other quarterbacks, Namath figured to have many productive passing years past 30. "When you get to the age of 30 if you've been able to survive the crises, you're really ready," Fran Tarkenton pointed out early in 1973. Tarkenton, after six seasons with the New York Giants, was traded to the Minnesota Vikings, where he had spent his first five seasons as a pro, in the summer of 1972.

"Len Dawson was better after 30," Tarkenton pointed out. "So was Jurgensen. So were Norm Van Brocklin and Y. A. Tittle. Namath will be. When you get to 30, you know the trouble spots, you know what you can do, and just as important, you know what you can't do."

Well known to almost everyone with an interest in pro football was the fact that Namath went past the 20,000-yard mark in 1972, after only eight seasons of pro competition. This was the earliest any quarterback in history had reached this plateau, achieved by only the greats of the game. Taking into consideration the fact that in two of Namath's first eight seasons, 1970 and 1971, he appeared in only nine games of a possible 28 overall, his 20,099 career passing yards after the 1972 campaign represented a remarkable achievement.

Football once was deemed incapable of producing a Babe Ruth, a folk hero of regal proportions. The nature of the game—in which great teams were called machines—had resulted in a non-player—the late, great Coach Vince Lombardi—becoming its dominant figure.

But Joe Namath, more than any other star in pro football's firmament during the years when the game was becoming, in the words of Pete Rozelle, "a $130,-000,000 business," proved that football's heroes could, indeed, be bigger than life.

It had to be Namath who, in an era when increasingly complex defenses were becoming the rule in pro football, routed the evolution of offensive strategy back on its course. As Joe put it: "Because of the development of the defenses, we've had to compensate and develop even more. When a guy runs out for a pass, he's not just running out for a pass. He reads what the coverage is, and I read what the coverage is, and we try to connect. When I go back to the huddle, I don't know what the pass is going to be. You have to read the weaknesses and strengths of the defense and take it from there."

No one has been able to take it as far as the man

from Beaver Falls. Winston Hill, a mountainous offensive tackle for the Jets, who served Namath magnificently as a pass protector for many seasons, perhaps best placed the quarterback in perspective.

"There won't be another one like him, with his talent and individualism," Hill said of Joe. "Not in this century."

JOE NAMATH'S COLLEGE AND PRO STATISTICS

UNIVERSITY OF ALABAMA

RUSHING

	Atts.	Yds.	Avg.	TD
1962	80	228	2.9	4
1963	76	211	2.8	5
1964	44	133	3.0	6
Totals	200	572	2.8	15

PASSING

	Atts.	Cmp.	Pct.	Yds.	TD	Int.
1962	146	76	.521	1192	12	8
1963	128	63	.492	765	8	7
1964	100	64	.640	757	6	4
Totals	374	203	.543	2714	26	19

NEW YORK JETS

RUSHING

	Atts.	Yds.	Avg.	TD
1965	8	19	2.4	0
1966	6	42	7.0	2
1967	6	14	2.3	0
1968	5	11	2.2	2
1969	11	33	3.0	2
1970	1	—1	—1.0	0
1971	3	—1	—0.3	0
1972	6	8	1.3	0
Totals	46	125	2.7	6

PASSING

	G.	Atts.	Cmp.	Pct.	Yds.	TD	Int.	Avg.
1965	14	340	164	.482	2220	18	15	6.53
1966	14	*471	*232	.493	*3379	19	*27	7.17
1967	14	*491	*258	.525	*4007	26	28	*8.16
1968	14	380	187	.492	3147	15	17	8.28
1969	14	361	185	.512	2734	19	17	7.57
1970	5	179	90	.503	1259	5	12	7.03
1971	4	59	28	.475	537	5	6	9.10
1972	14	324	162	.500	†2816	†19	21	8.69
Totals	93	2605	1306	.501	20,099	126	143	7.72

*Led American Football League
†Led American Football Conference
(Scored one touchdown in 1967 on fumble recovery)